"*Implementing Tootling Interventions* offers an empirically validated, class-wide intervention that is practical and relevant to the everyday work of educators. This book is a must read for any educator seeking to improve their students' prosocial behaviors leading to higher student engagement and learning in the classroom. This text equips educators with a powerful and highly effective peer-mediated tool to improve student behavior and support learning in the classroom. Its rich description of each of the components of tootling will leave educators feeling confident and ready to implement this intervention with fidelity."

Dr. Julie Fogt, *director, Centennial School of Lehigh University*

"*Implementing Tootling Intervention* is a very well written, informative, and a straightforward guide book for busy teachers. The book is structured in a way so that it is easy to go back and find the information you need to refresh your knowledge. So many great ideas, suggestions, and modifications are represented in this book. I can't wait to try this Tootling Intervention in my classroom!"

Michele Priebe, MS, *learning disabilities teacher for Waseca Public Schools*

"This book bridges the research to practice gap by prioritizing educational partnerships between students and teachers as well as emphasizing a positive and proactive classroom community."

Amanda Reinschmidt, Ed.S., NCSP, *school psychologist for over 10 years working in a variety of settings including middle school, high school, alternative high school, transition (18–21 program) settings, and residential settings*

"This book covers every aspect from setup, implementation, data collection, modifications/adaptations, fading to trouble shooting to ensure a successful outcome. Not that only is this intervention efficient and effective, it is equitable and centers on the student voice."

Emily Davis, Ed.S., NCSP, *school psychologist with over 10 years of elementary experience across four school districts in two states, serving low income and middle-class students and their families*

T0386491

Implementing Tootling Interventions

This book is a comprehensive guide to the history and implementation of the tootling intervention that was designed to increase prosocial behaviors in school-aged children.

Implementing Tootling Interventions provides practitioners with the resources and information needed to implement tootling effectively and successfully in their desired setting to increase prosocial behavior, decrease disruptive behavior, and increase academic engaged time for students. To address individuals of all abilities and ages, modifications are provided for early childhood education, elementary education, middle school, high school, special education, after-school programs, and more intensive behavioral settings. Specific components within tootling that lead to its effectiveness are discussed, along all the information and resources needed for this feasible, cost-effective intervention to be implemented.

This book is ideal for classroom teachers, school psychologists, social workers, or other school professionals looking for a practical and effective intervention to increase the prosocial behavior of their students.

Alexandra Hilt-Panahon is a professor of special education at Minnesota State University, Mankato. She earned her Ph.D. in School Psychology from Syracuse University and has worked in the field of education for over 25 years.

Kennedi Alstead is a practicing school psychologist with the St. Michael-Albertville school district in St. Michael, MN. She recently earned her Psy.D. in School Psychology from Minnesota State University, Mankato.

Implementing Tootling Interventions

A Practitioner's Guide to Increasing Peer Prosocial Behaviors

Alexandra Hilt-Panahon and Kennedi Alstead

NEW YORK AND LONDON

Designed cover image: Getty Image

First published 2023
by Routledge
605 Third Avenue, New York, NY 10158

and by Routledge
4 Park Square, Milton Park, Abingdon, Oxon OX14 4RN

Routledge is an imprint of the Taylor & Francis Group, an informa business

Library of Congress Cataloging-in-Publication Data
Names: Hilt-Panahon, Alexandra, author. | Alstead, Kennedi, author.
Title: Implementing tootling interventions : a practitioner's guide to increasing peer prosocial behaviors / Alexandra Hilt-Panahon, Kennedi Alstead.
Description: New York : Routledge, 2023. | Includes bibliographical references and index. |
Identifiers: LCCN 2022049141 (print) | LCCN 2022049142 (ebook) |
Subjects: LCSH: Behavior modification--United States. | Social skills--Study and teaching--Activity programs--United States. | Classroom management--United States.
Classification: LCC LB1060.2 .H55 2023 (print) | LCC LB1060.2 (ebook) | DDC 370.15/28--dc23/eng/20230103
LC record available at https://lccn.loc.gov/2022049141
LC ebook record available at https://lccn.loc.gov/2022049142

ISBN: 978-0-367-65268-5 (hbk)
ISBN: 978-0-367-65267-8 (pbk)
ISBN: 978-1-003-12866-3 (ebk)

DOI: 10.4324/9781003128663

Typeset in Baskerville
by Taylor & Francis Books

For Chip, Maura, and Caitlin – Alex

For my family, friends, and colleagues for their
tremendous support – Kennedi

Contents

Tables

Contributors

Lauren Arbolino, Ph.D. is a licensed School Psychologist with extensive clinical expertise across a wide range of professional environments. Dr. Arbolino has served as a classroom teacher, counselor, and school psychologist for public and private schools for over 20 years. She has worked as a behavior therapist, consultant, and teacher trainer. Dr. Arbolino received her Masters in Counseling (M.A.) from New York University and her Doctorate in School Psychology (Ph.D.) from Syracuse University. Her research examines academic and behavioral interventions for students with special needs and provides training to professionals to implement these interventions.

Acknowledgements

We would like to acknowledge all of the students, teachers, paraprofessionals, and other school personnel that we have worked with over the years. The lessons learned working in school settings were invaluable to the writing of this book. We would also like to thank Collin Seifert for his help preparing the manuscript for submission. Lastly, we would like to thank our friends and family who provided us support during the process of writing this book, we could not have done it without you.

Part I
History and Purpose

1   The History of Tootling

Alexandra Hilt-Panahon and Kennedi Alstead

The History of Tootling

Disruptive behavior in the classroom can have a negative impact on students' academic and social outcomes by interfering with classroom instruction (Hofstadter et al., 2009; Lambert et al., 2015; Lum et al., 2017). Additionally, these behaviors can lead to lower student achievement, both for the student creating the disruption and the other students in the classroom (Hofstadter et al., 2009; Lum et al., 2017). Unfortunately, many teachers continue to struggle with managing student behavior and promoting appropriate behavior in their classroom, even with the knowledge of the potential negative outcomes of disruptive behavior and difficulties with social skills (Cihak et al., 2009). In fact, it is more common for teachers to observe the negative behaviors that occur in the classroom as opposed to the positive, prosocial behaviors, which are viewed as expected behaviors (Akin-Little et al., 2004), due to the greater disruption to the classroom environment. Research also repeatedly demonstrates that teachers direct more of their attention to children with behavior problems; therefore, children who are rejected by peers are often teacher targets for corrective responses and feedback (Makowski, 2014). Another factor to consider is it is difficult for teachers to observe both the prosocial and negative behaviors due to the other demands on their time and attention, such as class-wide instruction and planning or other student needs (Lambert et al., 2015). Often then, this situation may lead to teachers relying on student reports on their classmates' behaviors (which are often negative), as well as a lack of opportunity for teachers to provide reinforcement for student prosocial behaviors (Cihak et al., 2009). This cycle creates a necessary demand for effective and efficient class-wide behavioral interventions to remediate these concerns in the classroom. This chapter will focus on the expected roles of the classroom teacher, confidence and training in classroom management, effective class-wide interventions, positive behavioral interventions, and peer-mediated interventions that aim to improve the overall classroom environment.

DOI: 10.4324/9781003128663-2

Roles of the Teacher

Teachers have a powerful role and influence on their students, whether that be positively or negatively (Makowski, 2014). Students tend to believe that teachers have higher authority than their parents when it comes to rules and practices, possibly due to the amount of time spent in school compared to at home during those school-age years. This increases the need for effective classroom management (Weber, 1999). How the teacher navigates and assumes their role as a teacher has an impact on the overall classroom community, classroom management strategies, and peer acceptance which emphasizes the importance of recognizing that how a teacher intervenes impacts the children in the classroom (Makowski, 2014).

Over the years, there have been assumptions of what the teacher's role is versus what their role actually entails. Teachers have the responsibility to focus their attention on instruction for all students in the classroom, which leaves little time to focus on all instances of problem behavior in the classroom (Lambert et al., 2015). Most teachers have to follow specific essential standards that all students must learn before the end of the school year. Many times, this is where the teacher's focus is and other things may fall through the cracks. Specifically, classroom management should be considered an equally important role for the teacher as it is a critical component in effective teaching (Piwowar et al., 2013). Without effective classroom management, there is no effective instruction (Ficarra & Quinn, 2014). Interestingly, one assumption of classroom management is that the teacher's responsibility is to maintain control over his/her students (Makowski, 2014). And yet, even though no one would argue the need for maintaining order and organization in the classroom as an essential component of effective teaching, emphasizing teacher control disregards the role that effective classroom management can have in contributing to students' moral and social development (Nucci, 2006).

Confidence and Training in Classroom Management

One reason for effective classroom management strategies being difficult for teachers to implement is preservice training for teachers in classroom management continuing to be an inadequate practice (Ficarra & Quinn, 2014). "Classroom management" is a term used regularly in education (Makowski, 2014). This over-arching concept includes behaviors and strategies teachers use to guide student behavior in the classroom (Evertson & Emmer, 1982). Misbehaviors, classroom disruptions, and social conflicts are inarguably challenging for some teachers. Therefore, traditionally, classroom management has been referred to as way of adults controlling students with punitive measures (i.e., "time-outs," suspensions, expulsions, etc.); however, recently there has been modifications to what classroom management entails. Evertson and Weinstein (2006) believe that classroom management has two distinct purposes: It not only seeks to establish and sustain an orderly environment so students can engage in meaningful academic learning, it also aims to enhance students' social and moral growth. These effective classroom management strategies are typically preventative and proactive; however, many teachers continue to rely on using fewer effective practices, such as aversive and reactive consequences for problem behavior due to their ease of implementation and immediate response (Dutton Tillery et al., 2010).

Only 18% of teachers report they learned classroom management skills as part of their teacher preparation program, and only 27% of these preparation programs offered a course on classroom management. The lack of preparation and training in classroom management for teachers in preservice training programs contributes to the lack of confidence of implementing effective behavior management strategies in the classroom. Researchers have conducted studies analyzing teachers' confidence in implementing these strategies. Gable et al. (2012) surveyed 3,060 general and special educators to determine their knowledge and skill level of working with students who engage in challenging behavior. Both general education and special education teachers portrayed they were either reluctant or unprepared to use evidence-based classroom management practices. Cooper et al. (2017) also surveyed 248 general and special educators on their experience with classroom management strategies. They discovered that general education teachers received significantly less training on classroom management compared to special education teachers. Teacher self-efficacy for classroom management is an important component of teachers' identity with implications for their teaching quality (Lazarides et al., 2020). It is also a major concern of most beginning teachers. Classroom management self-efficacy has been defined as teachers' judgment of their capability to effectively implement classroom management tasks during difficult times. Research shows that those who feel confident in their classroom management abilities report fewer classroom disruptions (Dicke et al., 2014).

In addition to confidence and training, it is important to understand the relationship between the teacher's response to problem behavior and the overall classroom community (Makowski, 2014). Typically, it is important for the teacher to respond immediately to a problem behavior in order to promote classroom management and set a precedent in their classroom. However, any way a teacher reacts after a behavior is a response, whether it be silence, ignoring, punishing, sending out of the classroom, or scolding. Additionally, the continued pattern of responses to behavior from the teacher leads to learned behavior of the students in the classroom. For example, if a student continues to get sent out of the classroom for not doing his work and being disruptive to the class, he may continue to avoid his work and disrupt the class if he is trying to escape the task/work. The teacher may also continue to send him out due to him being a distraction in the classroom. This leads to something known as the "negative reinforcement trap" that is commonly seen in school settings. Overall, the relationship between teacher response and classroom community can either have a positive or negative impact on effective classroom management. Without the knowledge and implementation of effective behavior management strategies, it is difficult to create a positive and productive classroom environment (Akin-Little et al., 2004).

To make matters more difficult, there is a lack of national standards on how to prepare teachers in classroom management (Evertson & Weinstein, 2006). Even with the available literature, handouts, and policies for teachers on classroom management, there is still a need for more proactive approaches and interventions (Makowski, 2014). Research shows effective classroom management increases students' academic engagement by having a positive impact on their attention, engagement, and motivation (Piwowar et al., 2013). However, effective classroom management continues to be one of the biggest challenges for teachers and also is one of the biggest factors for teacher burnout and job dissatisfaction (Friedman, 2006). Therefore, it is important for researchers and school personnel to continue to develop ways to assist with teachers' confidence in implementing effective classroom management strategies as well as providing them with evidence-based, positive, class-wide behavioral interventions that have been shown to improve the classroom environment and decrease problem behavior.

Class-Wide Interventions

Due to recent reforms in education, such as Response to Intervention (RtI), more schools are implementing more effective, universal interventions through Tier 1 service delivery (Hawkins, 2010). Tier 1 focuses on prevention and early intervention, as well as classroom management practices. This tier typically meets 80–90% of all student needs, with 10–20% of students still needing additional supports. The majority of these students' needs can be met through Tier 2 supports, which are more targeted interventions for groups of students with similar struggles. Those that do not respond to Tier 2 supports should then receive Tier 3 supports, which are more intensive, individualized interventions specific to the student.

Larger group settings, such as classrooms, are dynamic environments where teachers and students engage in many interactions with each other throughout a given school day (Conroy et al., 2008). Therefore, these environments provide a perfect opportunity for effective class-wide interventions, that typically fall within the Tier 1 service delivery and supports. Class-wide interventions lead to positive teacher-student interactions and promote student learning and engagement. Implementing universal classroom management practices and interventions can also reduce the amount of disruptive behavior in the classroom (Hirsch et al., 2019). Universal classroom management practices, such as class-wide behavioral interventions, are considered proactive measures to prevent problem behavior from occurring in the future and creating a positive learning environment (Hawkins, 2010; Martin et al., 2016). They are also classified as a group of research-based effective teaching strategies used positively and preventively to promote and reinforce social and behavioral competence in students while minimizing problem behaviors (Conroy et al., 2008).

Class-wide interventions are an efficient way to meet student needs rather than developing many individualized interventions that may require additional resources beyond what is available in the regular classroom (Hawkins, 2010). Some examples of class-wide behavioral interventions are as simple as providing frequent praise, providing opportunities to respond, and having classroom rules that serve as behavioral expectations (Conroy et al., 2008).

One specific class-wide intervention has been shown to significantly improve the classroom environment is the Good Behavior Game (Barrish et al., 1969). The Good Behavior Game rewards students for engaging in appropriate on-task behaviors during instructional times. During this intervention, the classroom is divided into two teams. A point is given to a team for any inappropriate behavior displayed by one of their team members. The goal is to have the fewest number of points at the end of the game, which is typically at the end of the day. The team that has the fewest number of points, wins a group reward. However, if both teams keep their points below a certain number, they both share the reward. This intervention has been shown to increase on-task behaviors and reduce disruptive behaviors in the classroom (Barrish et al., 1969; Harris & Sherman, 1973; Medland & Stachnik, 1972).

Positive Behavioral Interventions

In addition to class-wide interventions that focus on prevention of problem behaviors occurring in the future, positive behavioral interventions have also seen an increase in educational practices due to their effectiveness in decreasing problem behavior and increasing positive behavior from students (Bradshaw et al., 2010). The most common approach to classroom management focusing on building a school community is a positive, developmental view of children (Watson & Battistich, 2006). The connection between children's capacity for empathy and the importance of teachers viewing their students in a positive light is necessary (Makowski, 2014). Research shows that positive interactions between teachers and students helps to increase compliance and social skills in students (Hattie & Timperley, 2007). These are important developmental considerations to keep in mind when implementing positive behavioral interventions.

Research suggests that positive punishments, such as time outs, suspensions, expulsions and public reprimands are less effective that the implementation of positive and proactive forms of discipline (Makowski, 2014). Educators and other school professionals are beginning to understand this idea as well. This has led to a shift in the discipline and management of the classroom where educators are moving from traditional systems to attempting to demonstrate an engaging and caring environment. School districts and administrators are turning to preventative schoolwide models that focus on promoting a positive school environment and reducing discipline problems (Bradshaw et al., 2010). These models manage student behavior by laying out positive behavioral expectations, providing rewards to students who meet those expectations, and establishing a consistent strategy for managing student behavior problems (Sugai & Horner, 2006). One program that is commonly implemented in schools is Positive Behavioral Interventions and Supports (PBIS). This program contains three levels of supports that focus on preventing future behavioral problems by the strategies listed previously (Bradshaw et al., 2010). Research on PBIS has demonstrated effectiveness in sustained changes in schools' discipline practices and systems. In terms of behavioral outcomes, research shows PBIS is effective in increasing student perceptions of safety at school, increasing academic performance, decreasing office disciplinary referrals, decreasing students' need for school-based counseling services, and decreasing suspension rates.

Peer-Mediated Interventions

Recent research on positive behavioral interventions has included peer-mediated interventions, which are perhaps a more preventative and proactive approach for managing behaviors (Shelton-Quinn, 2009). It is often seen as unrealistic for general education teachers to implement individualized interventions for students while managing the rest of their responsibilities throughout a given school day (Collins et al., 2018). Peer-mediated interventions can be utilized as a more effective way of implementing interventions in the classroom. Within peer-mediated interventions, peers are the change agent leading to positive behavioral change, instead of continuously relying on teachers or other support staff to manage all of the behavioral interventions in the classroom. Students can be trained in these peer-mediated interventions to teach, reinforce, model, and encourage prosocial behaviors among their peers.

Peer-mediated interventions have been shown to improve students' academic, behavioral, social, and communicative behaviors (Collins et al., 2018). Specifically, they have been effective in improving academic achievement, decreasing disruptive behaviors, increasing on-task behaviors, and increasing students' social skills and self-esteem (Kaya et al., 2015). Effectiveness has been demonstrated across all ages from elementary to high school (Dunn et al., 2017). Using students as the change agents is more cost-effective, more generalizable, and less obtrusive in the classroom setting than interventions mediated by teachers (Shelton-Quinn, 2009). Using peer-mediated interventions also allows for immediate feedback and more opportunities to respond (Collins et al., 2018).

Some examples of peer-mediated interventions are class-wide peer tutoring, cooperative learning strategies, cross-age tutoring, peer tutoring dyads, peer-assisted learning strategies, peer assessment, peer modeling, and peer reinforcement (Dunn et al., 2017). Positive peer reporting (PPR) is another example of a peer-mediated intervention that uses students as change agent (Skinner et al., 2002). PPR is a class-wide social skills intervention that seeks to reinforce prosocial behaviors by having students publicly acknowledge their peers' appropriate behavior rather than inappropriate behavior. PPR was developed as a means of targeting children who are socially rejected or experience negative interactions with peers. Research has demonstrated the effectiveness of PPR on improving social interactions and prosocial behavior between peers, as well as in decreasing incidents of disruptive behavior in the classroom (Moroz & Jones, 2002; Skinner et al., 2002). Tootling, which is a variation of PPR, is considered a peer-mediated intervention because students are managing the intervention by writing tootles throughout the school day instead of the teacher being the interventionist (Cashwell et al., 2001; Skinner et al., 2000). PPR encourages general positive behavior to be reported, whereas in tootling, specific prosocial behaviors (e.g., helping a peer with their homework) are the focus.

Conclusion

Providing teachers and educators with effective class-wide, positive behavioral interventions has the ability to increase their confidence in classroom management and implementing interventions in their classroom. It also helps them prevent future problems by having the skills to implement preventative class-wide interventions in the coming years. Class-wide, positive, and peer-mediated interventions serve many purposes as demonstrated above. They are seen as efficient, resource friendly, and preventative. Tootling incorporates all three of these aspects. The variation of PPR, known now as tootling, was initially developed by Skinner et al. (2000). Tootling combines the effective practices listed above to increase academic engagement and prosocial behavior, and decrease disruptive behavior (Cihak et al., 2009; Lambert et al., 2015; Lum et al., 2017). Tootling will be discussed in further detail in the following chapters, focusing on its effective components, steps for implementation, and its evidence of effectiveness in increasing prosocial behavior and academic engagement, as well as decreasing disruptive behavior. Additionally, information will be provided regarding modifications for tootling within different populations and settings, troubleshooting the intervention, and fading the intervention. At the end, case studies will be discussed and evaluated that focuses on how tootling impacts behavior in the classroom, including information on the variables mentioned throughout the previous chapters.

References

Akin-Little, K. A., Little, S. G., & Gresham, F. M. (2004). Current perspective on school-based behavioral interventions: Introduction to the mini-series. *School Psychology Review*, 33(3), 323–325. https://doi.org/10.1080/02796015.2004.12086251.

Barrish, H. H., Saunders, M., & Wolf, M. M. (1969). Good behavior game: Effects of individual contingencies for group consequences on disruptive behavior in a classroom. *Journal of Applied Behavior Analysis*, 2(2), 119–124. https://doi.org/10.1901/jaba.1969.2-119.

Bradshaw, C., Mitchell, M., & Leaf, P. (2010). Examining the effects of schoolwide positive behavioral interventions and supports on student outcomes: Results from a randomized controlled effectiveness trial in elementary schools. *Journal of Positive Behavior Interventions*, 12(3), 133–148. https://doi.org/10.1177/1098300709334798.

Cashwell, T. H., Skinner, C. H., & Smith, E. S. (2001). Increasing second-grade students' reports of peers' prosocial behaviors via direct instruction, group reinforcement, and progress feedback: A replication and extension. *Education & Treatment of Children*, 24(2), 161–175. https://www.jstor.org/stable/42899652.

Cihak, D. F., Kirk, E. R., & Boon, R. T. (2009). Effects of classwide positive peer "tootling" to reduce the disruptive classroom behaviors of elementary students with and without disabilities. *Journal of Behavioral Education*, 18(4), 267–278. https://doi.org/10.1007/s10864-009-9091-8.

Collins, T. A., Hawkins, R. O., & Flowers, E. M. (2018). Peer-mediated interventions: A practical guide to utilizing students as change agents. *Contemporary School Psychology*, 22(3), 213–219. https://doi.org/10.1007/s40688-017-0120-7.

Conroy, M., Sutherland, K., Snyder, A., & Marsh, S. (2008). Classwide interventions: Effective instruction makes a difference. *TEACHING Exceptional Children*, 40(6), 24–30. https://doi.org/10.1177/004005990804000603.

Cooper, J. T., Gage, N. A., Alter, P., LaPolla, S., MacSuga-Gage, A. S., & Scott, T. (2017). Educators' self-reported training, use, and perceived effectiveness of evidence-based classroom management practices. *Preventing School Failure*, 62(1), 13–24. https://doi.org/10.1080/1045988X.2017.1298562.

Dicke, T., Parker, P. D., Marsh, H. W., Kunter, M., Schmeck, A., & Leutner, D. (2014). Self-efficacy in classroom management, classroom disturbances, and emotional exhaustion: A moderated mediation analysis of teacher candidates. *Journal of Educational Psychology*, 106(2), 569–583. https://doi.org/10.1037/a0035504.

Dunn, M. E., Shelnut, J., Ryan, J. B., & Katsiyannis, A. (2017). A systematic review of peer mediated interventions on the academic achievement of students with emotional/behavioral disorders. *Education and Treatment of Children*, 40(4), 497–524. https://doi.org/10.1353/etc.2017.0022.

Dutton Tillery, A., Varjas, K., Meyers, J., & Smith Collins, A. (2010). General education teachers' perceptions of behavior management and intervention strategies. *Journal of Positive Behavior*, 12(2), 86–102. https://doi.org/10.1177/1098300708330879.

Evertson, C. M., & Emmer, E. (1982). Preventative classroom management. In D. Duke (Ed.), *Helping teachers manage classrooms* (pp. 2–31). Association for Supervision and Curriculum Development.

Evertson, C. M., & Weinstein. C. S. (Eds.). (2006). *Handbook of classroom management: Research, practice, and contemporary issues*. Routledge.

Ficarra, L., & Quinn, K. (2014). Teachers' facility with evidence-based classroom management practices: An investigation of teachers' preparation programmes and in-service conditions. *Journal of Teacher Education for Sustainability*, 16(2), 71–87. https://doi.org/10.2478/jtes-2014-0012.

Friedman, I. A. (2006). Classroom management and teacher stress and burnout. In C. M. Evertson & C. S. Weinstein (Eds.), *Handbook of classroom management: Research, practice, and contemporary issues* (pp. 925–945). Routledge.

Gable, R. A., Tonelson, S. W., Sheth, M., Wilson, C., & Park, K. L. (2012). Importance, usage, and preparedness to implement evidence-based practices for students with emotional disabilities: A comparison of knowledge and skills of special education and general education teachers. *Education and Treatment of Children*, 35(4), 499–519. https://doi.org/10.1353/etc.2012.0030.

Harris, V. W., & Sherman, J. A. (1973). Use and analysis of the "Good Behavior Game" to reduce disruptive classroom behavior. *Journal of Applied Behavior Analysis*, 6(3), 405–417. https://doi.org/10.1901/jaba.1973.6-405.

Hattie, J., & Timperley, H. (2007). The power of feedback. *Review of Educational Research*, 77(1), 81–112. https://doi.org/10.3102/003465430298487.

Hawkins, R. O. (2010). Introduction to the special issue: Identifying effective classwide interventions to promote positive outcomes for all students. *Psychology in the Schools*, 47(9), 869–870. https://doi.org/10.1002/pits.20510.

Hirsch, S. E., Lloyd, J. W., & Kennedy, M. J. (2019). Professional development in practice: Improving novice teachers' use of universal classroom management. *The Elementary School Journal*, 120(1), 61–87. https://doi.org/10.1086/704492.

Hofstadter, K. L., Jones, K. M., & Therrien, W. J. (2009). Classwide effects of positive peer reporting on the on-task behavior of children with emotional disturbance. *Journal of Evidence-Based Practices for Schools*, 10(1), 2–19.

Kaya, C., Blake, J., & Chan, F. (2015). Peer-mediated interventions with elementary and secondary school students with emotional and behavioural disorders: A literature review. *Journal of Research in Special Education Needs*, 15(2), 120–129. https://doi.org/10.1111/1471-3802.12029.

Lambert, A. M., Tingstrom, D. H., Sterling, H. E., Dufrene, B. A., & Lynne, S. (2015). Effects of tootling on classwide disruptive and appropriate behavior of upper-elementary students. *Behavior Modification*, 39(3), 413–430. https://doi.org/10.1177/0145445514566506.

Lazarides, R., Watt, H. M. G., & Richardson, P. W. (2020). Teachers' classroom management self-efficacy, perceived classroom management and teaching contexts from beginning until mid-career. *Learning and Instruction*, 69, 1–14. https://doi.org/10.1016/j.learninstruc.2020.101346.

Lum, J. D. K., Tingstrom, D. H., Dufrene, B. A., Radley, K. C., & Lynne, S. (2017). Effects of tootling on classwide disruptive and academically engaged behavior of general-education high school students. *Psychology in the Schools*, 54(4), 370–384. https://doi.org/10.1002/pits.22002.

Makowski, E. M. (2014). From challenging behaviors to caring classroom communities: Reimagining the teacher's role in classroom management [Doctoral dissertation, University of Washington]. ProQuest Dissertations and Theses Global. https://www.proquest.com/dissertations-theses/challenging-behaviors-caring-classroom/docview/1703279113/se-2?accountid=12259.

Martin, N. K., Schafer, N. J., McClowry, S., Emmer, E. T., Brekelmans, M., Mainhard, T., & Wubbels, T. (2016). Expanding the definition of classroom management: Recurring themes and new conceptualizations. *Journal of Classroom Interactions*, 51(1), 31–41. https://www.jstor.org/stable/26174348.

Medland, M. B., & Stachnik, T. J. (1972). Good-behavior game: A replication and systematic analysis. *Journal of Applied Behavior Analysis*, 5(1), 45–51. https://doi.org/10.1901/jaba.1972.5-45.

Moroz, K. B., & Jones, K. M. (2002). The effects of positive peer reporting on children's social involvement. *School Psychology Review*, 31(2), 235–245. https://doi.org/10.1080/02796015.2002.12086153.

Nucci, L. (2006). *Classroom management for moral and social development*. In Everstein, C. M. & Weinstein. C. S. (Eds.), *Handbook of classroom management: Research, practice, and contemporary issues* (pp. 711–731). Routledge.

Piwowar, V., Thiel, F., & Ophardt, D. (2013). Training inservice teachers' competencies in classroom management. A quasi-experimental study with teachers of secondary schools. *Teaching and Teacher Education*, 30, 1–12. https://doi.org/10.1016/j.tate.2012.09.007.

Shelton-Quinn, A. D. (2009). Increasing positive peer reporting and on-task behavior using a peer monitoring interdependent group contingency program with public posting [Doctoral dissertation, Mississippi State University]. Mississippi State University Theses and Dissertations. https://scholarsjunction.msstate.edu/td/2687/.

Skinner, C. H., Cashwell, T. H., & Skinner, A. L. (2000). Increasing tootling: The effects of a peer-monitored group contingency program on students' reports of peers' prosocial behaviors. *Psychology in the Schools*, 37(3), 263–270. https://doi.org/10.1002/(SICI)1520-6807(200005)37:3<263::AID-PITS6>3.0.CO;2-C.

Skinner, C. H., Neddenriep, C. E., Robinson, S. L., Ervin, R., & Jones, K. (2002). Altering educational environments through positive peer reporting: Prevention and remediation of social problems associated with behavior disorders. *Psychology in the Schools*, 39(2), 191–202. https://doi.org/10.1002/pits.10030.

Sugai, G., & Horner, R. R. (2006). A promising approach for expanding and sustaining school wide positive behavior support. *School Psychology Review*, 35(2), 245–259. https://doi.org/10.1080/02796015.2006.12087989.

Watson, M., & Battistich, V. (2006). Building and sustaining caring communities. In C. M. Evertson & C. S. Weinstein (Eds.), *Handbook of classroom management: Research, practice, and contemporary issues* (pp. 253–279). Routledge.

Weber, E. K. (1999). Children's personal prerogative in home and school contexts. *Early Education and Development*, 10(4), 499–515. https://doi.org/10.1207/s15566935eed1004_5.

2 What is Tootling?

Alexandra Hilt-Panahon and Kennedi Alstead

What is Tootling?

As mentioned in the previous chapter, tootling is a peer-mediated, class-wide, positive behavioral intervention that has demonstrated effectiveness in decreasing disruptive behaviors and increasing prosocial behaviors as well as academic engagement in the classroom (Cashwell et al., 2001; Cihak et al., 2009; Lambert et al., 2015). The term "tootling" comes from the word "tattling" and the phrase "tooting your own horn" (Skinner et al., 2000). Instead of students reporting on their peers' negative behaviors, which is unfortunately commonly seen in the classroom, tootling encourages students to report on their peers' prosocial or positive behaviors (i.e., sharing with another student). This chapter will provide a deeper explanation of tootling, focusing on brief steps of implementation, rationale for its use, as well as the populations and target behaviors past research has focused on.

Brief Steps of Implementation

A more detailed discussion of the implementation steps of tootling will be held within Chapter 6; however, brief implementation steps will be provided within this chapter in order to gain a better understanding of what tootling looks like when implemented. When implementing the tootling intervention in a research context, the researchers will first train the cooperating teacher in the intervention. Training the teacher in the intervention usually consists of one short session of describing the intervention and providing a script for training the students. Once this is completed, the researchers and the teacher will train the students in the tootling process, using the script as a guide. Training the students includes instruction on what prosocial behaviors are, how and when to write a tootle, and how to earn their group reinforcement. Training the students consists of one to two sessions depending on how well the students understand the intervention. Once the students have been trained in the intervention, the researchers, teacher, and students agree on a set number of tootles needed to reach their goal. They also agree on a group reinforcement, to be awarded once the class reaches its goal.

DOI: 10.4324/9781003128663-3

After the training sessions, tootling is implemented in the classroom. Typically, students will write their tootles during designated transition or break times to not disrupt instruction. The teacher will read out loud the correct tootles that were written that day and provide oral feedback to the students who wrote the tootles and the students who were the recipients of the tootles. Corrective feedback is provided for incorrect tootles. This can be done at the end of the school day or the morning of the next school day depending on what is more feasible to the teacher. These tootles are then added to the cumulative total of tootles. This process is continued until the students reach the number of tootles specified in their goal. Once they have reached their goal, the class will receive their group reinforcement, the number of tootles starts back at zero, a new goal number of tootles is set, and a new group reinforcement is selected.

Rationale for Use

Tootling utilizes many aspects of effective interventions/programs that have demonstrated effectiveness in the past. For example, tootling is a class-wide intervention. As mentioned in the previous chapter, class-wide interventions have the ability to meet the needs of 80–90% of students, as well as providing those additional supports to students who may be struggling a little bit more compared to their peers (Hawkins, 2010). Class-wide interventions lead to positive relationships between the teacher and students while also promoting learning, academic engagement (Conroy et al., 2008), and reducing disruptive behavior (Hirsch et al., 2019) in a proactive manner (Martin et al., 2016). An additional appealing factor is that class-wide interventions, such as tootling, are an efficient way to meet student needs rather than developing individualized interventions for specific students (Hawkins, 2010).

Secondly, tootling is a positive behavioral intervention. As many school systems are turning to a more preventative model that focuses on fostering a positive school environment while also decreasing the number of disciplinary problems (Bradshaw et al., 2010), tootling fits in perfectly as it focuses on recognizing and reinforcing positive behaviors from peers/students. Tootling is a great class-wide intervention that falls within the Positive Behavioral Interventions and Supports (PBIS) model.

Lastly, tootling is a peer-mediated intervention, which means the students are the ones in charge of the behavioral change as they are the ones reporting on their peers' behaviors. Peer-mediated interventions are an effective way to implement interventions in the classroom instead of the teachers solely being in charge of implementation (Collins et al., 2018). Peer-mediated interventions have been shown to improve students' academic, behavioral, social, and communicative behaviors.

Past Research

Researchers have demonstrated tootling's effectiveness in increasing prosocial behaviors, increasing on-task behaviors, and decreasing disruptive behaviors in the general education classroom setting (Cashwell et al., 2001; Cihak et al., 2009; Lambert et al., 2015; Skinner et al., 2000). The majority of research on tootling has occurred in middle to upper elementary general education classroom settings, with more recent research extending tootling to other settings such as high school classrooms and after-school programs (Kirkpatrick et al., 2019; Lum et al., 2017). The following sections will discuss past research conducted on tootling in a variety of population and settings. The discussion of past research will be organized chronologically, so the reader has the ability to identify how the research on tootling has evolved through time. Specifically, the reader will be able to see how the effectiveness of tootling has been measured more efficiently and effectively in recent years, as well as the extension of the tootling intervention into other settings than the elementary general education classroom.

Populations and Settings

While most research on tootling has been conducted within elementary general education classroom settings, additional research has looked into the effectiveness of tootling within middle school classrooms, high school classrooms, after-school programs, and even with college students. Although the research in other settings is not as extensive, the results and details of these studies are important to mention. Information from these studies has helped the authors determine the best modifications for alternative settings as will be discussed within the chapters regarding the modification of tootling (Chapters 7–9).

Elementary School

Skinner et al. (2000) were the first to publish research on tootling, which they positioned as a modification of positive peer reporting (PPR). They implemented the tootling intervention with interdependent group contingencies and public posted feedback of their progress in a general education classroom consisting of 28 4th grade students (none receiving special education services). Using an ABAB withdrawal design, the students in the classroom exhibited increased reports of prosocial behaviors during the tootling intervention; however, the authors did not investigate the impact of tootling on student behaviors. The researchers published another study in which tootling was implemented in a 2nd grade general education classroom using an ABAB withdrawal design (again, none of the students received special education services; Cashwell et al., 2001). Their goal was to extend the tootling intervention to a younger group of students to investigate whether they could successfully participate in tootling. Thus, the dependent variable in this study was reports of prosocial behavior (tootles) rather than the behavior itself. In this study, the baseline phase was the tootling intervention without the interdependent group contingency component and public posted progress feedback and the intervention phase consisted of all three. During the intervention phase, reports of peer prosocial behavior increased, suggesting that 2nd grade students may be able to participate in tootling. In both of these early studies, the dependent variable is a limitation. Tootling may have only increased the reports of peer prosocial behavior rather than increasing the actual frequency of prosocial behavior.

Cihak et al. (2009) were the first to publish research on the effectiveness of tootling in decreasing disruptive behaviors in the classroom and were also the first in the published research to include students with disabilities. Although Morrison and Jones (2007) implemented class-wide positive peer reporting with a few students with disabilities, their dependent variables and implementation steps were quite different than the rest of the tootling research. Even though their results provide insight into positive peer reporting in general, a detailed discussion regarding their study will not be provided. Within the Cihak et al. (2009) study, tootling was implemented in one 3rd grade inclusive classroom that included four students with disabilities (SLD and/or ADHD) using an ABAB withdrawal design. Tootling was associated with a decrease in disruptive behaviors. The authors hypothesized that this was a result of increased positive reinforcement for prosocial behavior and possibly a decrease in reinforcement available for disruptive behavior. These researchers were also the first in the published literature to investigate the social validity of tootling. The classroom teacher reported favorable opinions about the tootling intervention and the improvements in students' behaviors.

Other studies have also investigated teacher acceptability of tootling. Lambert et al. (2015) implemented tootling in two general education classrooms, and both teachers rated it highly acceptable. In this study, researchers implemented tootling in two general education classrooms, one 4th grade classroom and one 5th grade classroom. The 5th grade classroom did not include students with disabilities; however, the 4th grade classroom included two students with a specific learning disability. These researchers used an ABAB withdrawal design with a multiple baseline element across classrooms and were the first to look at if tootling would also be effective in both decreasing disruptive behaviors and increasing rates of appropriate behaviors. Tootling was shown to be effective in decreasing class-wide disruptive behaviors and increasing appropriate behaviors across both classrooms. However, no data was collected regarding the effectiveness of the intervention specifically for the students with disabilities.

McHugh et al. (2016) furthered the tootling research for lower elementary general education classrooms. This study included three classrooms containing 2nd and 3rd grade students. One classroom contained no students receiving special education services, the second classroom contained three students receiving English as a Second Language services and were identified as having a disability under Other Health Impaired, and the third classroom had one student who received services under Other Health Impaired. There was one target student within each classroom that individual data would be collected on as the tootling intervention was taking place. None of these students were receiving special education services; however, they were all identified as demonstrating greater disruptive behavior than their peers. An ABAB withdrawal design was used in the three classrooms, along with a multiple baseline element across two of the classrooms. The purpose of this study was to determine the effectiveness of tootling on decreasing disruptive behavior and increasing academic engagement for the entire class, as well as individual target students' behavior. This is the first tootling study to look at the effectiveness of the behavioral intervention on an academic measure. Similarly, this study found that tootling was effective in decreasing class-wide and individual target student disruptive behavior. They also found that tootling increased class-wide and individual academically engaged behavior.

A more recent study conducted by McHugh Dillon et al. (2019) sought to evaluate the effect of tootling, with the modification of including ClassDojo technology on class-wide disruptive behavior and academically engaged behavior. This study included three 5th grade classrooms. Three students received special education services in the first classroom under Other Health Impaired and one student under Autism Spectrum Disorder. No students in the second classroom received special education services and five students in the third classroom received special education services under Specific Learning Disability and Other Health Impaired. Tootles were recorded through the use of the ClassDojo website and displayed to students via a projector. An ABAB withdrawal design in three classrooms was used. Results indicated that tootling with the use of ClassDojo technology is effective in decreasing disruptive behavior and increasing academically engaged behavior in the classroom.

Middle School

Tootling was most recently implemented in a middle school setting (Chaffee et al., 2020). This study sought to examine the effectiveness of tootling across two middle school classrooms on decreasing disruptive behavior and increasing academically engaged behavior. Two general education middle school classrooms participated in this study. One classroom had one student with a 504 plan for attention-deficit/hyperactivity disorder, and the other classroom had four students receiving special education services. Three of those students were receiving services under Other Health Impairment and one under Traumatic Brain Injury.

It was thought that the use of positive peer reporting within a middle school setting could have the potential of being rejected as students attempt to assert independence from adults and their own maturity this time. However, it was also thought that this may be a perfect time to implement such an intervention due to the prime time of social pressure and self-growth. This study demonstrated that tootling was effective in increasing academic engaged behavior and decreasing disruptive behavior in each middle school classroom.

High School

Until recently, tootling has mostly been implemented in elementary general education classrooms. Previous researchers had mentioned that future research should be conducted to determine if public prosocial comments may be embarrassing to older students (Cihak et al., 2009; Lambert et al., 2015). There had been concerns about the effectiveness of tootling for this population. The effectiveness of tootling in secondary settings was first addressed by a group of researchers who implemented tootling in three high school general education classrooms using an ABAB withdrawal design with follow-up in each of the three classrooms (Lum et al., 2017). The researchers did not specify if any of the students in the three classrooms had a disability, but all three classrooms were chosen based on high levels of disruptive behavior. Tootling was shown to be effective in decreasing class-wide disruptive behaviors and increasing on-task behavior across classrooms. The results from this study are important because it is the first example of published literature of implementing tootling in high school general education classrooms, which provides an initial indication that it may be effective among older students. Additionally, the researchers identified an effect of tootling on academically engaged behaviors.

In 2019, Lum et al. conducted another study that examined the effects of tootling on three high school general education classrooms in decreasing disruptive behavior and increasing academically engaged behavior. Three students in the first classroom received special education services for Specific Learning Disability, no students in the second classroom received special education services, and four students in the third classroom received special education services for Specific Learning Disability and one received services for Other Health Disabilities. A withdrawal design was used for all three classrooms. This time, a randomized independent group contingency was used to reward students instead of an interdependent group contingency. Teachers, at the end of the class, drew three submitted tootles and rewarded the students for whom the tootle was written about. They also drew the names of two students who wrote a tootle and rewarded them as well. All three classrooms had decreases in disruptive behavior and increases in academically engaged behavior in their classrooms during the tootling phases. This study suggests that a modified tootling procedure can be used as an effective intervention for teachers to improve the behavior in their high school classrooms.

After-School Program

An additional extension of the tootling research was conducted by Kirkpatrick et al. (2019). This study sought to determine if tootling decreased antisocial/disrespectful interactions of four, teacher-nominated, 3rd grade students in an after-school setting. This after-school program consisted of students who were considered "at-risk" and who were frequently mean and disrespectful to each other and staff. There were academic activities and other non-academic activities throughout the day.

The intervention was implemented in a 3rd grade classroom which included 18 students. Direct observation was collected on four African American students, two boys and two girls. None of the four students were receiving special education services, but three were receiving additional reading instruction.

The tootling intervention was implemented during the academic hour of the day, which included 20 minutes spent on a carpet where the teacher reviewed upcoming activities and provided teacher-led instruction. After this, the class broke into groups and participated in stations targeting different academic skills. However, data was only collected during the carpet time because it was consistently delivered and provided opportunities for students to interact.

Results from this study showed that tootling decreased antisocial/disrespectful behaviors in an after-school setting, during an academic period. Specifically, this relationship was demonstrated through four, 3rd grade students that have been identified as having problem behaviors. This study was intended to be different from tootling interventions within the typical school day in several ways. For example, activities and routines were more varied, consequences for inappropriate behavior were less consistent, students were mixed with other students not in their typical classrooms, teachers were part-time volunteers, and researchers were responsible for implementing the intervention.

College Students

One study has been conducted on the use of tootling in a post-secondary setting (Lipscomb et al., 2018). Tootling was implemented in a comprehensive transitional program at a major university with seven emerging adult students with intellectual disabilities. This study evaluated the effectiveness of using ClassDojo alone and ClassDojo in combination with tootling. The researchers found that ClassDojo alone was more effective in reducing problem behavior in the classroom as a whole and with most individual students. However, the combination of ClassDojo and tootling was also effective in comparison with baseline measures.

Students With Disabilities

There is little information regarding its effectiveness with students with disabilities. Although several studies have included students with disabilities in the classroom (i.e., SLD and ADHD), there has been little data collected solely on how tootling affects the behavior of students with disabilities (Cihak et al., 2009; Lambert et al., 2015).

Target Behaviors

Initial tootling studies used increased reports of prosocial behaviors (tootles) during the tootling intervention as their dependent variable (Skinner et al.,

2000; Cashwell et al., 2001) instead of observing its effects on prosocial behavior, disruptive behavior, and on-task behavior. However, researchers later started to use observable behaviors as their dependent measures, as tracking reports of tootles does not determine whether or not tootling increased the rates of prosocial behavior in the classroom (Cihak et al., 2009; Lambert et al., 2015; Lum et al., 2017). These studies demonstrated tootling's effectiveness in increasing prosocial behaviors and on-task behaviors, as well as decreasing disruptive behaviors in the classroom.

Prosocial Behavior/Appropriate Behavior

The research on the increase of prosocial behaviors began with counting the number of instances of peers helping classmates that were reported each day (tootles; Skinner et al., 2000). The authors of this study mention how measuring the number of tootles is only the first step in determining the effectiveness of the intervention in changing behavior. However, the following study conducted by Cashwell et al. (2001), used the same measure of prosocial behavior. It wasn't until Lambert et al.'s study in 2015 that appropriate behavior was measured as an observable behavior; however, this definition is later used within the academically engaged behavior section. Appropriate behavior was defined as the student being actively involved or attending to independent seatwork, teacher instruction, designated classroom activities, and/or engaging in task-related vocalizations with teachers and/or peers. They found that tootling is effective in increasing appropriate behavior in the classroom. One major limitation of this is that the definition of appropriate behaviors includes much more than prosocial behaviors. No study has yet to use an observational measure of prosocial behavior to determine the impact of tootling on increasing the rate of prosocial behavior in the classroom.

Disruptive/Antisocial/Inappropriate Behavior

Cihak et al. (2009) were the first researchers to determine the effectiveness of tootling in decreasing disruptive behaviors. Their dependent variable, specifically, was the total number of disruptive behaviors performed by the entire class. The disruptive behaviors were defined as any student demonstrating at least one of the following behaviors: talking out, out of seat without teacher's permission, and engaging in any motor behavior that interfered with another student's studying. The teacher collected data regarding disruptive behavior for the entire school day by using a bracelet made from construction paper that contained all the initials of the students in her classroom. Tallies were made next to the student's name that engaged in those behaviors.

The mean number of daily disruptive behaviors per students across baseline and interventions phases were also recorded (Cihak et al., 2009). It is of importance to note that the students with disabilities had a higher mean number of daily disruptive behaviors within the first baseline phase compared to students without disabilities. This pattern continued throughout all phases. Within the first tootling phase, students with disabilities had a decrease in daily disruptive behaviors, followed by an increase within the second baseline phase, and finally, a decrease within the second tootling phase. More importantly, this demonstrates an initial identification that tootling may be effective for students with disabilities.

Lambert et al. (2015) also defined their disruptive behaviors as a student demonstrating at least one of the following: out of seat without permission, inappropriate vocalizations, and engaging in any physical, motor movements unrelated to the task at hand. They also found that tootling was effective in decreasing disruptive behavior in the classroom. Chaffee et al. (2020) used the same operational definition of disruptive behavior for their study.

McHugh et al. (2016) defined disruptive behaviors as a student exhibiting one or more of the following: inappropriate vocalizations, out of seat/area, or playing with objects. These behaviors were specifically chosen since they encompassed a wide variety of behaviors that the teachers indicated to be most problematic in their classrooms. Their latter study in 2019 also used the same definition for class-wide disruptive behaviors.

Lum et al. (2017) determined the disruptive behaviors by using a modified Problem Identification Interview (Kratochwill & Bergan, 1990). They determined the three most frequent disruptive behaviors in the class according to each teacher. All three teachers chose inappropriate vocalizations, being out of seat, and playing with objects. Lum et al. (2019) used the same procedures to determine the three most frequent disruptive behaviors in the high school classrooms. All three teachers again chose being out of seat, inappropriate vocalizations, and playing with objects as the most frequent behaviors that disrupted their class.

Kirkpatrick et al. (2019) defined their antisocial/disruptive interactions as a student engaging in disrespectful or aggressive behaviors directed toward staff or other students, such as physical aggression, verbal aggression, disrespectful interactions and/or body language, statements of rejection, accusing or blaming peers, interrupting or speaking while a peer or teacher is speaking, and preventing peers from joining in games or other activities.

On-Task/Academically Engaged

McHugh et al. (2016) were the first researchers to measure the effects of tootling on academically engaged behaviors. They defined academically engaged behaviors as the student actively involved or participating in independent seatwork, group activities, and/or attending to teacher instruction, which may require vocalizations relevant to the task. Before each observation session, the teachers informed the students of the expected behaviors to be engaged in. The students were counted as being academically engaged when they were following these directions. Additionally, their latter study in 2019 used a similar definition of academically engaged behavior for their study, which included a student attending to teacher instruction or participating in independent seatwork and group activities.

Lum et al. (2017) measured academically engaged behavior as well and defined it as the student being actively involved or attending to independent seatwork, teacher instruction, designated classroom activities, and/or engaging in task related vocalizations with teacher and/or peers. The same operational definition of academically engaged behavior was used for their second study in 2019. However, an additional measure of academically engaged behavior was the measurement of passive off-task behavior. This was defined as the student not attending to the assigned task in an academically engaged manner, without being disruptive.

Chaffee et al. (2020) used both passive and active academic engagement within their operational definition. Active engagement was defined as when the student was actively involved with academic tasks and/or speaking with a teacher or peer about the assigned material. Passive engagement was defined as attending to the assigned work.

Evidence of Effectiveness

As one may be able to interpret, there is a growing body of literature that supports the use of tootling as a class-wide intervention to meet the needs of most students. Therefore, is important to evaluate if this literature base demonstrates tootling as an evidence-based practice. This section will focus on the current available literature and tools used to determine the qualification for tootling as an evidence-based practice. The authors conducted an extensive review of the literature and used available criteria to inform their decision.

In recent decades, educators have begun to formulate guidelines to identify evidence-based practices that should be implemented in the educational setting to help students become more successful (Cook et al., 2014). School settings have also begun to emphasize the importance of empirically-based research in their schools and implement practices that have been proven to not only be effective, but that produce successful outcomes for learners in the general education setting and the special education setting. Bridging the research-to-practice gap is a prominent theme in contemporary special education reforms. For example, the No Child Left Behind Act of 2001 and the Individuals with Disabilities Education Improvement Act (IDEA) of 2004 both emphasize using research as the basis of training and practice.

Previous to this realization, educational research had been applied haphazardly in schools, and the gap between research and practice was even more problematic within special education (Slavin, 2002). Teachers often gravitated to simple interventions found on teacher blogs (e.g., Teachers pay Teachers) and social media (Grote-Garcia & Vasinda, 2014). These are widely available to all educators and easy to access, but they may not have the research to support their use compared to interventions that are outlined within educational journals. An evidence-based intervention is an intervention that has been studied and has demonstrated reliability across multiple studies and has had consistent results (Cook et al., 2014). Rather than relying on findings from one, potentially flawed study, research consumers should identify effective practices that use experimental research designs and demonstrate robust effects on student outcomes. This is the benefit of an evidence-based practice. Although effective, evidence-based practices can be deemed as more costly (i. e., time and resources), which may impact the amount of buy-in from school personnel; however, it is important for all to understand the long-lasting benefits of implementing an evidence-based intervention with their students such as positive and consistent results.

The Council for Exceptional Children (CEC) worked to determine classification of practices as evidence-based based on specific criteria and qualifications. Due to tootling being a newer intervention and the current amount of available research, the authors determined that conducting a best-evidence synthesis would increase buy-in from educators and other professionals who may be interested in implementing positive behavioral interventions. As of now, there has been no research conducted on the use of these practices outlined by the CEC in identifying tootling as an evidence-based practice. The authors used these guidelines to determine if tootling should be considered an evidence-based practice.

After reviewing the current literature base, evaluating 11 different tootling articles, and applying specific criteria to determine if tootling meets the expectations of an evidence-based practice, the researchers determined that tootling should be considered an evidence-based practice. Although it is understood that tootling is a growing and developing intervention, there is promise in its effectiveness to create positive behavior change for the majority of students. However, the tootling research base is still limited in the fact that most of the research conducted was in the general education classroom and little individual results were reported on students with varying disabilities. This suggests that the authors do not assert that tootling is an evidence-based practice for students with disabilities in special education classrooms, given the lack of methodologically sound studies in those areas.

The confirmation of tootling as an evidence-based practice, with general education students, holds significant implications for practice. Given the recent attention towards implementing evidence-based practices within a school setting, a positive class-wide behavioral intervention, such as tootling, is significant. Based on the evidence from this study and each of the individual studies analyzed within this review, tootling should be considered for use in lower elementary through postsecondary settings as an effective class-wide intervention to remediate disruptive behavior and improve academic engagement for all students. However, it should be noted that the majority of the research on tootling has been conducted in elementary general education classroom settings, whereas the research on tootling in middle school, high school, and postsecondary settings is limited. Additionally, the existing literature also points to the need for research exploring the effectiveness of tootling with special education populations outside of the general education classroom.

Another implication for practice is the feasibility of implementing this class-wide, positive behavioral intervention within an already established School-Wide Positive Behavior Intervention and Supports system, as this intervention focuses on recognizing positive behavior of peers and includes class-wide rewards for achieving a class goal. In addition, tootling can be used as a universal, Tier 1 intervention for an entire class, while also being used as a Tier 2 intervention by providing additional supports for the students within the classroom that may be struggling with behavioral problems.

Finally, the tootling intervention provides a proactive, class-wide approach to a variety of common classroom problems. The intervention is simple to implement, is acceptable to teachers who implement, and can be adapted to a variety of age groups and settings. Given these positive aspects of the intervention, it is important to "get the word out" about this intervention so that more teachers adopt its use in their classroom.

Limitations

Tootling has demonstrated effectiveness in the general education classroom setting on a variety of behaviors, including prosocial behavior, disruptive behavior, and academic engagement, and at a variety of age levels, from 2nd grade to college-level students. However, as previously mentioned, there is little to no research regarding its effectiveness among students with disabilities (Cihak et al., 2009; Lambert et al., 2015; Lum et al., 2017) either in the general education classroom setting or in a special education classroom setting. Several studies included students with disabilities in their study; however, the researchers did not run a separate analysis for these students due to the small sample size of students with disabilities in their studies.

Additionally, researchers have yet to identify the causal mechanism(s) of tootling, or in other words, the most important component(s) of tootling (Cihak et al., 2009; Lambert et al., 2015; Lum et al., 2017). Since tootling is a multicomponent intervention, it is important for researchers to analyze how each of the components contributes to the effectiveness of tootling in increasing prosocial behaviors and decreasing disruptive behaviors in classrooms. Specifically, researchers have not separated the effects of the components of peer tootling which have been previously shown to be effective on their own in improving behavior: the peer mediated nature of tootling, the interdependent group contingency, multiple components of effective feedback, and the training procedures. One previous study investigated the effect of adding the interdependent group contingency component, which may provide additional reinforcement for students' reports of their peers' prosocial behaviors (Cashwell et al., 2001). However, these researchers only examined how adding the group contingency component to tootling affected the number of tootles that were reported, not the actual occurrence of prosocial and disruptive behaviors. Other components within tootling have not been analyzed separately.

Future Directions

Tootling has demonstrated effectiveness across general education classroom settings in increasing prosocial behavior, decreasing disruptive behavior and improving time on-task (Cashwell et al., 2001, Cihak et al., 2009; Lambert et al., 2015; Lum et al., 2017; Skinner et al., 2000). Even though there is evidence to support the effectiveness of tootling as a behavioral intervention, additional research is still needed needed to identify tootling as an evidence-based intervention. In fact, Chapter 4 will take the readers through the process the authors used to determine if tootling is an evidence-based intervention.

In order to address the limitations mentioned previously, future research should investigate the effectiveness of tootling in increasing prosocial behaviors and decreasing disruptive behaviors for students with a wide range of disabilities. As the number of students with disabilities increases, specifically students with behavioral problems, the more important it is for researchers to investigate positive behavioral interventions that address these behaviors (Conroy et al., 2008). Therefore, future studies should continue to evaluate the effectiveness of tooling in different settings other than the general education classroom, such as special education classrooms, alternative education classroom settings, or juvenile detention center settings. Additional research could also evaluate the effectiveness of tootling for students with specific disabilities, such as Emotional/Behavioral Disorders, Autism Spectrum Disorder, or Attention-Deficit/Hyperactivity Disorder. This will facilitate the generalization of the intervention to a wider variety of settings and populations.

Since tootling is a multicomponent intervention, future research should address the effectiveness of each of these components in the intervention. Specifically, research should analyze the separate impact of the peer-mediation component, the training procedures utilized, the interdependent group-oriented contingency, and the feedback component. As mentioned previously, each of these components has beneficial contributions to the intervention, but each should be evaluated to understand the main components of behavioral change from tootling. For example, previous research has shown that interdependent group contingencies were the most effective in controlling disruptive behavior in a classroom compared to independent and dependent group contingencies (Gresham & Gresham, 1982). Therefore, it is important that future research analyze the separate components of tootling on the rates of prosocial and disruptive behaviors. The next chapter will discuss the research that supports the effectiveness of the components of tootling previously mentioned in past research.

References

Bradshaw, C., Mitchell, M., & Leaf, P. (2010). Examining the effects of schoolwide positive behavioral interventions and supports on student outcomes: Results from a randomized controlled effectiveness trial in elementary schools. *Journal of Positive Behavior Interventions*, 12(3), 133–148. https://doi.org/10.1177/1098300709334798.

Cashwell, T. H., Skinner, C. H., & Smith, E. S. (2001). Increasing second-grade students' reports of peers' prosocial behaviors via direct instruction, group reinforcement, and progress feedback: A replication and extension. *Education & Treatment of Children*, 24(2), 161–175. https://www.jstor.org/stable/42899652.

Chaffee, R. K., Briesch, A. M., Volpe, R. J., Johnson, A. H., & Dudley, L. (2020). Effects of a class-wide positive peer reporting intervention on middle school student behavior. *Behavioral Disorders*, 45(4), 224–237. https://doi.org/10.1177/0198742919881112.

Cihak, D. F., Kirk, E. R., & Boon, R. T. (2009). Effects of classwide positive peer "tootling" to reduce the disruptive classroom behaviors of elementary students with and without disabilities. *Journal of Behavioral Education*, 18(4), 267–278. https://doi.org/10.1007/s10864-009-9091-8.

Collins, T. A., Hawkins, R. O., & Flowers, E. M. (2018). Peer-mediated interventions: A practical guide to utilizing students as change agents. *Contemporary School Psychology*, 22(3), 213–219. https://doi.org/10.1007/s40688-017-0120-7.

Conroy, M., Sutherland, K., Snyder, A., & Marsh, S. (2008). Classwide interventions: Effective instruction makes a difference. *TEACHING Exceptional Children*, 40(6), 24–30. https://doi.org/10.1177/004005990804000603.

Cook, B., Buysse, V., Klingner, J., Landrum, T., McWilliam, R., Tankersley, M., & Test, D. (2014). CEC's standards for classifying the evidence base of practices in special education. *Remedial and Special Education*, 36(4), 220–234.

Gresham, F. M., & Gresham, G. N. (1982). Interdependent, dependent, and independent group contingencies for controlling disruptive behavior. *The Journal of Special Education*, 16(1), 101–110. https://doi.org/10.1177/002246698201600110.

Grote-Garcia, S., & Vasinda, S. (2014). Pinning and practice: Using Pinterest as a tool for developing pedagogical content knowledge. *Texas Journal of Literacy Education*, 2(1), 36–45.

Hawkins, R. O. (2010). Introduction to the special issue: Identifying effective classwide interventions to promote positive outcomes for all students. *Psychology in the Schools*, 47(9), 869–870. https://doi.org/10.1002/pits.20510.

Hirsch, S. E., Lloyd, J. W., & Kennedy, M. J. (2019). Professional development in practice: Improving novice teachers' use of universal classroom management. *The Elementary School Journal*, 120(1), 61–87. https://doi.org/10.1086/704492.

Kirkpatrick, B. A., Wright, S., Daniels, S., Taylor, K. L., McCurdy, M., & Skinner, C. H. (2019). Tootling in an after-school setting: Decreasing antisocial interactions in at-risk students. *Journal of Positive Behavior Interventions*, 21(4), 228–237. https://doi.org/10.1177/1098300719851226.

Kratochwill, T.R., & Bergan, J. R. (1990). *Behavioral consultation in applied settings: An individual guide*. Plenum Press.

Lambert, A. M., Tingstrom, D. H., Sterling, H. E., Dufrene, B. A., & Lynne, S. (2015). Effects of tootling on classwide disruptive and appropriate behavior of upper-elementary students. *Behavior Modification*, 39(3), 413–430. https://doi.org/10.1177/0145445514566506.

Lipscomb, A. H., Anderson, M., & Gadke, D. L. (2018). Comparing the effects of ClassDojo with and without Tootling intervention in a postsecondary special education classroom setting. *Psychology in the Schools*, 55(10), 1287–1301. https://doi.org/10.1002/pits.22185.

Lum, J. D. K., Radley, K. C., Tingstrom, D. H., Dufrene, B. A., Olmi, D. J., & Wright, S. J. (2019). Tootling with a randomized independent group contingency to improve high school classwide behavior. *Journal of Positive Behavior Interventions*, 21(2), 93–105. https://doi.org/10.1177/1098300718792663.

Lum, J. D. K., Tingstrom, D. H., Dufrene, B. A., Radley, K. C., & Lynne, S. (2017). Effects of tootling on classwide disruptive and academically engaged behavior of general-education high school students. *Psychology in the Schools*, 54(4), 370–384. https://doi.org/10.1002/pits.22002.

Martin, N. K., Schafer, N. J., McClowry, S., Emmer, E. T., Brekelmans, M., Mainhard, T., & Wubbels, T. (2016). Expanding the definition of classroom management: Recurring themes and new conceptualizations. *Journal of Classroom Interactions*, 51(1), 31–41. https://www.jstor.org/stable/26174348.

McHugh Dillon, M. B., Radley, K. C., Tingstrom, D. H., Dart, E. H., & Barry, C. T. (2019). The effects of tootling via ClassDojo on student behavior in elementary classrooms. *School Psychology Review*, 48(1), 18–30. https://doi.org/10.17105/SPR-2017-0090.V48-1.

McHugh, M. B., Tingstrom, D. H., Radley, K. C., Barry, C. T., & Walker, K. M. (2016). Effects of tootling on classwide and individual disruptive and academically engaged behavior of lower-elementary students. *Behavioral Interventions*, 31, 332–354. https://doi.org/10.1002/bin.1447.

Morrison, J. Q., & Jones, K. M. (2007). The effects of positive peer reporting as a class-wide positive behavior support. *Journal of Behavioral Education*, 16(2), 111–124. https://doi.org/10.1007/s10864-006-9005-y.

Skinner, C. H., Cashwell, T. H., & Skinner, A. L. (2000). Increasing tootling: The effects of a peer-monitored group contingency program on students' reports of peers' prosocial behaviors. *Psychology in the Schools*, 37(3), 263–270. https://doi.org/10.1002/(SICI)1520-6807(200005)37:3<263::AID-PITS6>3.0.CO;2-C.

Slavin, R. E. (2002). Evidence-based education policies: Transforming educational practice and research. *Educational researcher*, 31(7), 15–21.

3 Components of Tootling

Alexandra Hilt-Panahon and Kennedi Alstead

Components of Tootling

As mentioned in the previous chapters, tootling is a class-wide, positive behavioral intervention with multiple components that contribute to successful implementation and effectiveness (Skinner et al., 2000). These components are: (a) the peer-mediation aspect, (b) the training procedures, (c) the interdependent group-oriented contingency component, and (d) the multiple aspects of feedback included in the intervention. Each of these will be discussed in turn, focusing on the effectiveness of each practice as documented in research.

Peer-Mediation

As mentioned in the first chapter of this book, recent research on positive behavioral interventions has included peer-mediated interventions, which have become an option for a more preventative and proactive approach for managing behaviors due to the students being the intervention change agent (Shelton-Quinn, 2009). General education teachers have many roles throughout their given school day; therefore, many teachers have expressed that the effort and time it takes to implement the individualized interventions it takes to ensure all students in their classroom are successful is often a tough thing to manage (Collins et al., 2018). Implementing interventions where peers are the change agent, instead of having teachers or other support staff manage all of the behavioral interventions in the classroom, allows for a more efficient and less time intensive avenue for positive behavioral change (Shelton-Quinn, 2009). Students can be trained in these peer-mediated interventions to teach, reinforce, model, and encourage prosocial behaviors among their peers. These interventions have improved students' academic, behavioral, social, and communicative behaviors (Collins et al., 2018). Specifically, they have been effective in improving academic achievement, decreasing disruptive behaviors, increasing on-task behaviors, and increasing students' social skills and self-esteem (Kaya et al., 2015). Using peer-mediated interventions also allows for immediate feedback and more opportunities to respond (Collins et al., 2018).

DOI: 10.4324/9781003128663-4

Some examples of peer-mediated interventions are class-wide peer tutoring, cooperative learning strategies, cross-age tutoring, peer tutoring dyads, peer-assisted learning strategies, peer assessment, peer modeling, and peer reinforcement (Dunn et al., 2017). As mentioned previously, tootling was derived from a previously well-researched intervention known as positive peer reporting, which is also a peer-mediated intervention. Tootling is considered a peer-mediated intervention because students are managing the intervention by writing tootles throughout the school day instead of the teacher being the interventionist. Students select their peers they would like to write a tootle on, they are observing the prosocial behavior, and they are in charge of when they reach their own selected tootle goal. The teacher manages the intervention, but the students are the ones that are implementing the intervention daily.

Training Procedures

Another component that contributes to the effectiveness of tootling is the training procedure that occurs before the intervention begins. When conducting tootling as a research study, the researcher would first train the classroom teacher in the intervention (Skinner et al., 2000). This varies depending on the researchers; however, it involves explaining to the teacher what the intervention is, what it entails, and how they should train the classroom. The classroom teacher is commonly provided a script to guide them through training their students in the intervention (Lambert et al., 2015). If tootling is not implemented as a research study, then the classroom teacher or individual interested in implementing the intervention, would follow our implementation guidelines in Chapter 6: How to Implement Tootling. Next, the teacher (and researchers) trains the students on the tootling procedures, including training on what prosocial behaviors are, examples of prosocial behaviors that constitute a tootle, how to report tootles, and providing time for the students to practice giving their own oral examples of prosocial behaviors with corrective feedback and praise given when appropriate. The students can also practice writing tootles on the tootling card, including who engaged in the prosocial behavior, what the prosocial behavior was, and who it benefitted. Oral praise and corrective feedback are again given to the students who have written example tootles after the examples are read aloud by the teacher. Giving the students time to write tootles allows the interventionist to gauge who needs more instruction in tootling and in what areas. Or, it allows the interventionist to determine if the students are ready to move on to implementation.

As mentioned previously, training the students can take up to two separate sessions. Past researchers have conducted two 20-minute training sessions focusing on how to report their peers' prosocial behaviors (Cashwell et al., 2001; Cihak et al., 2009). The first session consisted of the students defining and providing examples of prosocial behaviors. The teacher followed up by explaining different types of prosocial behaviors and describing a prosocial behavior in detail, with examples and non-examples of prosocial behaviors. Students were then asked to raise their hand and provide additional examples and corrective feedback was provided by the teacher (Cashwell et al., 2001). The second session consisted of the teacher instructing the students on how to write examples of peer prosocial behaviors on index cards (i.e., a correct tootle; Cihak et al., 2009). Then, students were asked to write their own examples. After these were written, the teacher provided corrective feedback when there were errors and provided praise when the students wrote accurate tootles. It is not uncommon for students to be asked to write a multitude of tootle examples to demonstrate they are aware of how to participate in the intervention. After the second session, the students were told the next school day they would find index cards on their desk and that these would be used to record the tootles (Cashwell et al., 2001). Lambert et al. (2015) only conducted one training session for the students where all steps were included during the one training session and it continued until all students successfully wrote one correct tootle. Both of these training procedures have been shown to be effective, and often the factor of time may constitute if one or two sessions would be best for training.

Explicit instruction, including opportunities to respond, and behavioral skills training are the key components within the tootling training procedures. Teachers use explicit instruction during tootling training to teach students about prosocial behaviors. Explicit instruction for the development and improvement of social skills has been a topic of interest for many years (Ashdown & Bernard, 2012). Explicit instruction is defined as

> a group of research-supported instructional behaviors used to design and deliver instruction that provides needed supports for successful learning through clarity of language and purpose, and reduction of cognitive load. It promotes active student engagement by requiring frequent and varied responses followed by appropriate affirmative and corrective feedback and assists long-term retention through use of purposeful practice strategies.
>
> (Hughes et al., 2017, p. 143)

Some researchers believe younger children will not benefit from direct, explicit instruction of social and emotional skills (Ashdown & Bernard, 2012); however, other researchers have documented effectiveness of social and emotional learning programs that include formal lessons for children during the preschool years (Payton et al., 2008) throughout secondary education for older children (Bernard, 2007). In fact, the most successful social-emotional learning programs use a direct, systematic, and explicit method for teaching skills (Joseph & Strain, 2003). Students that are taught these skills using explicit instruction have demonstrated improvements in social skills and decreases in disruptive or problem behavior. During tootling training, teachers use explicit instruction practices to teach the students about prosocial behaviors, providing frequent opportunities for students to respond (as discussed below), and giving students frequent feedback throughout the training process.

One effective component of explicit instruction is providing opportunities to respond (Hughes et al., 2017). Opportunities to respond are defined as an instructional question, statement, or gesture made seeking a response from students which can be written, oral or gestural (Fitzgerald Leahy et al., 2019). Opportunities to respond in the classroom have been shown to increase academic engagement as well as increase appropriate student behavior and decrease disruptive behavior. Including this component in the tootling training procedures increases the students' engagement to better learn the tootling process. For example, the teacher asks the students for examples of prosocial behavior after being taught what a prosocial behavior is (Skinner et al., 2000). Additionally, students are given opportunities to respond through the writing of their practice tootles.

Finally, the tootling training procedures include aspects of behavioral skills training to instruct, model, rehearse and provide feedback about tootling and prosocial behaviors (Hassan et al., 2018). Behavioral skills training has been used to teach a variety of skills across a variety of populations. Among these skills are a variety of social skills, such as increasing conversation skills and negotiating and giving compliments. Acquiring information about and understanding prosocial behaviors needed for tootling is a novel skill for many children, and behavioral skills training has been shown to be effective in teaching these novel skills in a very brief period of time and is viewed as an important aspect in implementing many behavioral interventions (Dogan et al., 2017).

Interdependent Group-Oriented Contingency

Another component of tootling is the interdependent group contingency (Skinner et al., 2000). During the training days, the class decides on a total number of tootles needed to receive a class-wide reward. The students, in collaboration with the classroom teacher, decide on the reward that will be earned by reaching the predetermined number of tootles. Tootling aids in cooperation within the classroom by having all students work together to reach a common goal. Once the students reach their predetermined number of tootles, the entire class earns their reward and the number of tootles resets to zero and the process repeats, beginning with the teacher and students determining another goal and interdependent group contingency.

Group-oriented contingencies have been shown to be an effective and efficient way to manage student behaviors (McKissick et al., 2010). There are three types of group-oriented contingency programs that can be implemented to increase appropriate behavior and decrease inappropriate behavior by students: independent, dependent, and interdependent group-oriented contingencies (Skinner et al., 2004). These types of group-oriented contingency programs differ in how students are reinforced based on individual and group performance. Independent group-oriented contingencies consist of individuals receiving rewards based on their own behaviors meeting a criterion; however, the target behaviors, criteria, and rewards are the same for all students. Dependent group-oriented contingencies consist of all individuals receiving or not receiving access to a reward based on an individual student's or the behaviour of a few students; therefore, the access to the reinforcement is not based on a student's own behavior, but that of a select few in the larger group. Finally, interdependent group-oriented contingencies involve an entire group/ classroom earning a reward based on the entire group meeting a specified goal or criterion. In this case, the access to the reward is based on the individual's behavior as well as their classmates.

Copious amounts of research have supported the evidence to support the effectiveness of using contingent rewards to enhance the quality of performance for children (Skinner et al., 2004). Specifically, when children are given access to reinforcers that are contingent upon performance of a target behavior or meeting a criterion, they exhibit improved performance in these areas. Group-oriented contingency programs have been shown to decrease disruptive behavior across a wide range of students from preschool to high school, as well as students with disabilities (Ling et al., 2011). It has been demonstrated that educators can increase the probability that students will choose to engage in appropriate behaviors by improving the rates, quality and immediacy of the reinforcement for the appropriate behaviors as well as decreasing the rate of inappropriate behaviors (Skinner et al., 2004).

One common difficulty with reinforcement programs, such as group contingencies is that many educators disagree with providing tangible rewards contingent upon positive behavior (Skinner et al., 2004). Additionally, there are concerns with students consistently not meeting the criterion and becoming frustrated (Ling et al., 2011). However, there are many beneficial aspects to implementing a group-oriented contingency program in a classroom setting. For example, these interventions require less time and effort for teachers because students are receiving a reward based on a group contingency, not a contingency for a specific individual. Second, students are not singled out and reinforced for the appropriate behavior related to their individual contingency. Finally, group-oriented contingencies use peer influence and attention as a way to improve classroom behaviors and decrease unwanted, inappropriate behaviors.

There has been research to demonstrate the additional benefits of using an interdependent group-oriented contingency (which tootling utilizes) over the other two types of group-oriented contingency programs (Ling et al., 2011). This type of contingency encourages students to work together to reach a common goal or reward. This enables cooperation and increased prosocial interactions between the students in the classroom. It has also been identified as easier to implement for teachers since only one contingency is in place and all students receive the same reward based on the performance of their entire group. Additionally, interdependent group-oriented contingencies reduce the possibility of jealousy and peer rejection since the entire group either receives the award or not based on the entire group performance (Murphy et al., 2007). Interdependent group-oriented contingency program has demonstrated effectiveness in decreasing disruptive behaviors and increasing on-task behaviors for students of a variety of grade levels (Ling et al., 2011).

Researchers have examined the effectiveness of a class-wide intervention alone and the class-wide intervention combined with an interdependent group-oriented contingency component (Lo & Cartledge, 2004). Specifically, these researchers were looking at the difference in effectiveness between a total class peer tutoring intervention and the interdependent group-oriented contingency on social studies performance and off-task behaviors for students in the 4th grade. When examining the effects of the total class peer tutoring intervention alone as well as combined with the interdependent group contingency, no clear differences were found between the two interventions, but both interventions led to improved social studies performance and decreased off-task behaviors. Limitations for this study were addressed, and additional research needs to be done to determine the difference in effectiveness for including interdependent group contingencies for other class-wide interventions. Tootling uses the interdependent group contingency to increase the motivation of students to engage in the intervention by writing tootles (Lum et al., 2017).

Feedback

A final component of tootling is the provision of feedback, both through public posting of progress toward group contingencies and oral feedback from the teacher (Skinner et al., 2000). Daily progress toward the goal number of tootles is tracked using visual representation of tootles (i.e., a thermometer tracking the number of tootles needed to reach their goal, a clear container in which students place their tootles). The visual representation allows students to see their progress toward receiving the interdependent group-oriented contingency. Students should be able to see their progress towards their goal in order to provide additional reinforcement and encouragement for prosocial behaviors to occur (Cashwell et al., 2001). Additionally, teachers at the end of the school day or the beginning of the following school day reads aloud some of the tootles that were written and provides oral performance feedback to the students who wrote the tootles and the students that engaged in the prosocial behavior.

Feedback is one of the most influential factors in changing behavior, learning, and achievement (Hattie & Timperley, 2007). Feedback can be defined as "information provided by an agent regarding aspects of one's performance or understanding" (Hattie & Timperley, 2007, p. 81). Performance feedback that contains elements of praise, immediacy, specificity, and public posting of progress have been shown to be effective in improving positive behaviors as well as academic achievement (Van Houten et al., 1975). Feedback is considered most effective when it is visually presented, auditorily presented, or computer-assisted; and relates to specific goals that have been set (Hattie & Timperley, 2007). In addition, feedback has been found to be more effective when it provides information on correct responses rather than incorrect responses as well as when the goals set by the classroom are specific and challenging, but the complexity of the task is low.

By including feedback into the classroom environment, classroom behavior can improve dramatically (Hattie & Timperley, 2007). Tootling incorporates effective feedback components of specificity, immediacy, public posting, and positive reinforcement throughout the implementation of the intervention. Each of these elements will be discussed in the following sections.

Specific Feedback

Research shows that feedback must be specific to the task, process, and performance of the individual or group. Specifically, the feedback should address the following questions: (1) Where am I going? (2) How am I going? (3) Where to next? (Hattie & Timperley, 2007). First, the specific feedback given should address where the students need to go in order to be successful. This can be done through setting challenging but specific goals. By setting a goal, students know where they need to be and can monitor their performance in order to reach this goal. Second, in providing feedback on how a student is going, the teacher should provide information related to the task at hand or a performance goal that has been set. Lastly, in providing feedback to address where to next, the teacher can provide information that allows for greater possibilities for learning, such as greater self-regulation of the task, fluency of the task, and an increased understanding of the task. Each of these three questions should be answered when providing specific feedback to give students information about their performance, specifying what was done well, what needs improvement, and how to improve (Elliot et al., 2000).

Specific feedback has been found to be effective in many settings and for many groups. For example, researchers have shown that providing written and specific comments on exams is more effective than solely providing the grade on the exam (Black & William, 1998). This has been shown to improve the test performance of students compared to grades alone (Page, 1958). Researchers have examined the effects of different forms of feedback, including specific positive feedback, specific negative feedback, non-specific positive feedback, non-specific negative feedback, and no feedback (Orluwene & Ekin, 2015). They found that students who received specific feedback, whether positive or negative, improved significantly on academic related tasks than those who received non-specific feedback. This corresponds with other findings on specific feedback being more effective in enhancing learning in the classroom (Chase & Houmanfar, 2009). Specific feedback allows for students to understand how they performed and how they can improve (Orluwene & Ekin, 2015).

In tootling, teachers provide orally administered specific feedback on progress toward the class goal, and students provide specific, positive written feedback (tootles) about the prosocial behaviors they observe. Tootling also incorporates the three questions that feedback should address. First, the classroom agrees on a specific goal they need to reach to receive their reward as a whole; therefore, the classroom is aware of where they are going. This goal is determined based on performance of the classroom in achieving the previous goal. Second, the teacher provides corrective feedback and specific praise on the student written tootles to help students determine how they are going. This includes how the entire class is doing to achieve their class-wide goal as well as the individual tootles that are written. Finally, the "where to next?" aspect of feedback is addressed by students using this information to self-monitor their implementation of the intervention as well as an increased fluency of the task as the intervention continues and feedback is provided by the teacher.

Immediacy of Feedback

There is substantial research regarding the effectiveness of immediate versus delayed feedback (Hattie & Timperley, 2007). The research indicates that immediate feedback may be most beneficial at the process level and delayed feedback may be most effective at the task level. Feedback at the process level addresses the processes needed to understand or perform a task. Feedback at the task level involves how well tasks are understood and performed. During tootling, task level feedback is provided in a delayed fashion by the teacher, typically given the following day regarding written tootles. The teacher provides feedback at the task level to assist students in their understanding of how well the task was understood and performed, such as whether tootles were written correctly and how many tootles were recorded toward the goal. This type of feedback is helpful in encouraging students to write more correct tootles. Additional research demonstrates that although immediate feedback is effective in modifying student behavior, feedback that is presented up to a day later is also effective in improving social behavior of students (Ragland et al., 1981). Researchers implementing tootling may want to consider additional ways immediate feedback at the process level can be added to the intervention to increase the effectiveness of feedback.

Public Posting of Progress Feedback

Feedback is most effective when it provides information regarding students' progress toward reaching their goal (Hattie & Timperley, 2007). Research has also found public posting of feedback effective in improving positive behavior in a variety of settings and for a variety of individuals (Van Houten et al., 1975), such as psychiatric aides, tutors, teachers, and elementary school students (Van Houten & Van Houten, 1977). It is also seen as a simple and effective way to manage classroom behavior. One study documented how publicly posting the names of children who returned to class quickly after recess led to a decrease in the number of students who were late for class (Hall et al., 1970). Research also shows how posting both individual and team/class performance is more effective than posting just individual performance (Van Houten & Van Houten, 1977). Finally, public posting of progress was also linked to an increase in on-task behaviors and an increase in feedback from peers (Kastelen et al., 1984). Students were also interested in seeing how they were performing based on the posted feedback, which demonstrates the social validity of public posting of progress feedback. Progress toward the group's interdependent group contingency is publicly posted in the tootling intervention, which according to past research should be motivating for students and help them reach their goal.

Individual-Focused Positive Reinforcement/Praise

Students participating in tootling receive positive reinforcement for appropriate, prosocial behaviors in many different ways. Specifically, students receive a reward for reaching their goal number of tootles through the interdependent group contingency described above, which is a tangible form of positive reinforcement and involves the entire class receiving a reward to increase appropriate behavior. The other major aspect of positive reinforcement that the students receive during tootling is oral praise from their teacher for engaging in the prosocial behavior that another student reported on as well as writing a correct tootle (Skinner et al., 2000). In addition, they receive positive written praise from their peer through the written tootle. This section will focus on how individual students receive oral praise from the classroom teacher and written praise from their peers for writing correct tootles and engaging in prosocial behaviors to increase appropriate and desired behavior by the students.

Before the recent focus on reinforcing positive behavior, punishment was generally seen as the best way to remediate disruptive or inappropriate behavior (Horner & Macaya, 2018). Punishment can be defined as the addition of an aversive stimulus or the removal of a reinforcing stimulus that decreases the probability of a behavior occurring (Miltenberger, 2016). Positive reinforcement is the addition of a reinforcing stimulus that increases the probability of the behavior occurring again in the future. Originally, educators believed that positive reinforcement was too time-intensive, not rewarding enough for the teachers, and socially unacceptable (Maag, 2001). Punishment was more acceptable to teachers because it was easier to implement, despite the copious amounts of research documenting the effectiveness of positive reinforcement. Punishment strategies have also been shown to be both ineffective and expensive ways to deal with problem behavior (Horner & Macaya, 2018). Alternatives, such as a focus on reinforcing positive behavior and teaching positive social skills, are effective in managing and reducing the occurrence of problem behavior. Additionally, by teaching positive social skills, acknowledging when students engage in positive behaviors, and positively reinforcing those positive behaviors, students that were at risk for problem behavior show improved emotional regulation.

Overall, positive reinforcement leads to decreased problem behavior and improved prosocial behavior as well as an increase in academic achievement for all students (Reinke et al., 2007). Specific interventions that focus on positive reinforcement, such as token economies, behavioral contracts, and group-oriented contingencies are considered effective research-based interventions for reducing problem behaviors (Maag, 2001). Additional research has demonstrated the effectiveness of teachers using oral praise in improving social skills and academic performance (Reinke et al., 2013). Specifically, oral praise from teachers has been shown to increase appropriate behavior of disruptive students, decrease off-task behavior, decrease disruptive behavior, and increase academic engagement of all students (Reinke et al., 2007; Reinke et al., 2013). However, in order for this type of praise to be effective, it must be specific toward the effort, self-regulation, engagement, or processes related to the task and its performance (Hattie & Timperley, 2007). Setting challenging and specific goals for the classroom to achieve also increases the effectiveness of oral feedback. With a more specific goal, feedback by the teacher can be more directly linked to that goal and can include information on how to achieve the goal. Additionally, oral praise increases the intrinsic motivation of students by helping them feel more confident in their abilities (Reinke et al., 2007). By increasing positive interactions with students, even the most challenging students demonstrate improvements in compliant and positive behavior. Not only do teachers have the ability to modify behavior through praise, students may also positively reinforce one another through facial expressions, comments, or subtle gestures (Maag, 2001). Peers' capacity to reinforce one another is beneficial when implementing a peer-mediated intervention.

It is important for teachers to be consistent and deliberate in their acknowledgement and reinforcement of positive behavior, such as through oral praise (Reinke et al., 2013). Catching students being good for engaging in positive behaviors is one simple way to decrease problem behaviors as opposed to expecting students to behave "as they should" (Maag, 2001). Indeed, positive reinforcement is effective in reducing a wide range of problem behaviors including behaviors that are maintained by negative reinforcement, such as escape from a non-preferred task (Payne & Dozier, 2013; Schieltz et al., 2019). This realization is important since teachers prefer positive reinforcement over negative reinforcement because it is less disruptive to learning (Maag, 2001). Positive reinforcement has also been shown to be more effective than negative reinforcement in decreasing problem behavior and increasing compliant behavior (Payne & Dozier, 2013). Additionally, researchers have shown that students generally prefer positive reinforcement (in this case, tangible items) for positive behavior over negative reinforcement (in this case, escape from a nonpreferred situation). Given its effectiveness and preference by teachers and students, positive reinforcement is likely ideal in many cases.

Feedback Within Tootling

Tootling utilizes multiple effective forms of feedback. For example, positive reinforcement is provided through oral praise by the teacher, written praise by peers, and when students achieve their goal and earn the interdependent group-oriented contingency. Peer feedback has been found to be effective in improving class performance (Van Houten & Van Houten, 1977). In fact, peer-mediated feedback provides many benefits in improving positive social behavior from students (Ragland et al., 1981). These benefits include peers being a cost-free resource that are plentiful in a classroom environment and being time-efficient due to feedback alone being able to produce behavioral change from peers. When peers as well as adults in the classroom serve as sources of feedback, the rate of feedback and the classroom environment may improve. Students writing tootles of their peers' prosocial behaviors contributes to the increased opportunity for feedback and the increased rate of behavior change. Secondly, feedback regarding the class's progress in achieving their goal is presented visually through a visual indicator, such as a classroom thermometer. Thirdly, the feedback regarding their progress toward their goal is provided by the visual progress indicator as well as comments from the teacher regarding their progress toward their goal the following day. The goal set by the students and the teacher is typically a specific and challenging goal to achieve; however, the difficulty of the task of writing a tootle is low, which assists in the effectiveness of progress feedback. Fourthly, tootling does not contain specific elements of immediate feedback, but due to the intervention being at the task level, delayed feedback is still considered an effective way to present the feedback to contribute to the behavior change. Finally, the teacher provides only feedback regarding correct tootles rather than commenting on incorrect tootles which is also an effective feedback practice.

Conclusion

The multiple evidence-based components of tootling drive its effectiveness in positive behavioral change. From using peers as the intervention agents to accessing effective components of feedback, tootling has demonstrated its success in increasing academic engagement and decreasing in disruptive behavior in a multitude of settings and populations. Although tootling is a newer intervention, there are several studies that will be analyzed and discussed in the next chapter. Through the process of conducting a best-evidence synthesis, the authors will determine if tootling should be considered a best-evidence practice and intervention.

References

Ashdown, D., & Bernard, M. (2012). Can explicit instruction in social and emotional learning skills benefit the social-emotional development, well-being, and academic achievement of young children? *Early Childhood Education Journal*, 39(6), 397–405. https://doi.org/10.1007/s10643-011-0481-x.

Bernard, M. E. (2007). *Program achieve: A social and emotional learning curriculum* (3rd ed.). Australian Scholarships Group.

Black, P., & William, D. (1998). Assessment and classroom learning. *Assessment in Education: Principles, Policy & Practice*, 5(1), 7–74. https://doi.org/10.1080/0969595980050102.

Cashwell, T. H., Skinner, C. H., & Smith, E. S. (2001). Increasing second-grade students' reports of peers' prosocial behaviors via direct instruction, group reinforcement, and progress feedback: A replication and extension. *Education & Treatment of Children*, 24(2), 161–175. https://www.jstor.org/stable/42899652.

Chase, J.A., & Houmanfar, R. (2009). The differential effects of elaborate feedback and basic feedback on student performance in a modified, personalized system of instruction course. *Journal of Behavioral Education*, 18(3), 245–265. https://doi.org/10.1007/s10864-009-9089-2.

Cihak, D. F., Kirk, E. R., & Boon, R. T. (2009). Effects of classwide positive peer "tootling" to reduce the disruptive classroom behaviors of elementary students with and without disabilities. *Journal of Behavioral Education*, 18(4), 267–278. https://doi.org/10.1007/s10864-009-9091-8.

Collins, T. A., Hawkins, R. O., & Flowers, E. M. (2018). Peer-mediated interventions: A practical guide to utilizing students as change agents. *Contemporary School Psychology*, 22(3), 213–219. https://doi.org/10.1007/s40688-017-0120-7.

Dogan, R., King, M., Fischetti, A., Lake, C., Mathews, T., & Warzak, W. (2017). Parent implemented behavioral skills training of social skills. *Journal of Applied Behavior Analysis*, 50(4), 805–818. https://doi.org/10.1002/jaba.411.

Dunn, M. E., Shelnut, J., Ryan, J. B., & Katsiyannis, A. (2017). A systematic review of peer mediated interventions on the academic achievement of students with emotional/behavioral disorders. *Education and Treatment of Children*, 40(4), 497–524. https://doi.org/10.1353/etc.2017.0022.

Elliot, S. N., Kratochwill, T. R., Cook, J. I., & Travers, J. F. (2000). *Educational psychology: Effective teaching, effective learning* (3rd ed.). McGraw Hill.

Fitzgerald Leahy, L. R., Miller, F. G., & Schardt, A. A. (2019). Effects of teacher-directed opportunities to respond on student behavioral outcomes: A quantitative synthesis of single-case design research. *Journal of Behavioral Education*, 28(1), 78–106. https://doi.org/10.1007/s10864-018-9307-x.

Hall, R. V., Cristler, C., Cranston, S. S., & Tucker, B. (1970). Teachers and parents as researchers using multiple baseline designs. *Journal of Applied Behavior Analysis*, 3(4), 247–255. https://doi.org/10.1901/jaba.1970.3-247.

Hassan, M., Simpson, A., Danaher, K., Haesen, J., Makela, T., & Thomson, K. (2018). An evaluation of behavioral skills training for teaching caregivers how to support social skill development in their child with autism spectrum disorder. *Journal of Autism and Developmental Disorders*, 48(6), 1957–1970. https://doi.org/10.1007/s10803-017-3455-z.

Hattie, J., & Timperley, H. (2007). The power of feedback. *Review of Educational Research*, 77(1), 81–112. https://doi.org/10.3102/003465430298487.

Horner, R. H., & Macaya, M. M. (2018). A framework for building safe and effective school environments: Positive Behavioral Interventions and Supports (PBIS). *Pedagogická orientace*, 28(4), 663–685. https://doi.org/10.5817/PedOr2018-4-663.

Hughes, C. A., Morris, J. R., Therrien, W. J., & Benson, S. K. (2017). Explicit instruction: Historical and contemporary contexts. *Learning Disabilities Research & Practice*, 32(3), 140–148. https://doi.org/10.1111/ldrp.12142.

Joseph, G. E., & Strain, P. S. (2003). Comprehensive evidence-based social-emotional curricula for young children: An analysis of efficacious adoption potential. *Topics in Early Childhood Special Education*, 23(2), 62–73. https://doi.org/10.1177/02711214030230020201.

Kastelen, L., Nickel, M., & McLaughlin, T. F. (1984). A performance feedback system: Generalization of effects across tasks and time with eighth-grade English students. *Education & Treatment of Children*, 7(2), 141–155. https://www.jstor.org/stable/42898842.

Kaya, C., Blake, J., & Chan, F. (2015). Peer-mediated interventions with elementary and secondary school students with emotional and behavioural disorders: A literature review. *Journal of Research in Special Education Needs*, 15(2), 120–129. https://doi.org/10.1111/1471-3802.12029.

Lambert, A. M., Tingstrom, D. H., Sterling, H. E., Dufrene, B. A., & Lynne, S. (2015). Effects of tootling on classwide disruptive and appropriate behavior of upper-elementary students. *Behavior Modification*, 39(3), 413–430. https://doi.org/10.1177/0145445514566506.

Ling, S., Hawkins, R. O., & Weber, D. (2011). Effects of a classwide interdependent group contingency designed to improve the behavior of an at-risk student. *Journal of Behavioral Education*, 20(2), 103–116. https://doi.org/10.1007/s10864-011-9125-x.

Lo, Y., & Cartledge, G. (2004). Total class peer tutoring and interdependent group oriented contingency: Improving the academic and task related behaviors of fourth-grade urban students. *Education and Treatment of Children*, 27(3), 235–262. https://www.jstor.org/stable/42900545.

Lum, J. D. K., Tingstrom, D. H., Dufrene, B. A., Radley, K. C., & Lynne, S. (2017). Effects of tootling on classwide disruptive and academically engaged behavior of general-education high school students. *Psychology in the Schools*, 54(4), 370–384. https://doi.org/10.1002/pits.22002.

Maag, J. W. (2001). Rewarded by punishment: Reflections on the disuse of positive reinforcement in schools. *Exceptional Children*, 67(2), 173–186. https://doi.org/10.1177/001440290106700203.

McKissick, C., Hawkins, R. O., Lentz, F. E., Hailley, J., & McGuire, S. (2010). Randomizing multiple contingency components to decrease disruptive behaviors and increase student engagement in an urban second-grade classroom. *Psychology in the Schools*, 47(9), 944–959. https://doi.org/10.1002/pits.20516.

Miltenberger, R. G. (2016). *Behavior modification: Principles and procedures* (6th ed.). Cengage Learning.

Murphy, K. A., Theodore, L. A., Aloiso, D., Alric-Edwards, J. M., & Hughes, T. L. (2007). Interdependent group contingency and mystery motivators to reduce preschool disruptive behavior. *Psychology in the Schools*, 44(1), 53–63. https://doi.org/10.1002/pits.20205.

Orluwene, G. W., & Ekin, R. E. D. (2015). Differential effects of feedback types on the improvement on students' performance in school-based assessment. *International Journal of Development and Emerging Economics*, 3(1), 10–25. https://www.eajournals.org/

journals/international-journal-of-developing-and-emerging-economies-ijdee/vol-3issue-1-march-2015/differential-effects-feedback-types-improvement-students-performance-school-based-assessment/.

Page, E. B. (1958). Teacher comments and student performance: A seventy-four classroom experiment in school motivation. *Journal of Educational Psychology*, 49(4), 173–181. https://doi.org/10.1037/h0041940.

Payne, S. W., & Dozier, C. L. (2013). Positive reinforcement as treatment for problem behavior maintained by negative reinforcement. *Journal of Applied Behavior Analysis*, 46(3), 699–703. https://doi.org/10.1002/jaba.54.

Payton, J., Weissberg, R. P., Durlak, J. A., Dymnicki, A. B., Taylor, R. D., Schellinger, K. B., & Pachan, M. (2008). *The positive impact of social and emotional learning for kindergarten to eighth-grade students: Findings from three scientific reviews*. Collaborative for Academic, Social, and Emotional Learning (CASEL). http://www.mentalhealthprom otion.net/resources/packardes.pdf.

Ragland, E. U., Kerr, M. M., & Strain, P. S. (1981). Social play of withdrawn children: A study of the effects of teacher-mediated peer feedback. *Behavior Modification*, 5(3), 347–359. https://doi.org/10.1177/014544558153004.

Reinke, W. M., Herman, K. C., & Stormont, M. (2013). Classroom-level positive behavior supports in schools implementing SW-PBIS: Identifying areas for enhancement. *Journal of Positive Behavior Interventions*, 15(1), 39–50. https://doi.org/10. 1177/1098300712459079.

Reinke, W. M., Lewis-Palmer, T., & Martin, E. (2007). The effect of visual performance feedback on teacher use of behavior-specific praise. *Behavior Modification*, 31(3), 247–263. https://doi.org/10.1177/0145445506288967.

Schieltz, K. M., Wacker, D. P., Suess, A. N., Graber, J. E., Lustig, N. H., & Detrick, J. (2019). Evaluating the effects of positive reinforcement, instructional strategies, and negative reinforcement on problem behavior and academic performance: An experimental analysis. *Journal of Developmental and Physical Disabilities*, 32(2), 339–363. https://doi.org/10.1007/s10882-019-09696-y.

Shelton-Quinn, A. D. (2009). Increasing positive peer reporting and on-task behavior using a peer monitoring interdependent group contingency program with public posting [Doctoral dissertation, Mississippi State University]. Mississippi State University Theses and Dissertations. https://scholarsjunction.msstate.edu/td/2687/.

Skinner, C. H., Cashwell, T. H., & Skinner, A. L. (2000). Increasing tootling: The effects of a peer-monitored group contingency program on students' reports of peers' prosocial behaviors. *Psychology in the Schools*, 37(3), 263–270. https://doi.org/ 10.1002/(SICI)1520-6807(200005)37:3<263::AID-PITS6>3.0.CO;2-C.

Skinner, C. H., Williams, R. L., & Neddenriep, C. E. (2004). Using interdependent group oriented reinforcement to enhance academic performance in general education classrooms. *School Psychology Review*, 33(3), 384–397. https://doi.org/10.1080/ 02796015.2004.12086255.

Van Houten, R., Hill, S., & Parsons, M. (1975). An analysis of a performance feedback system: The effects of timing and feedback, public posting, and praise upon academic performance and peer interaction. *Journal of Applied Behavior Analysis*, 8(4), 449–457. https://doi.org/10.1901/jaba.1975.8-449.

Van Houten, R., & Van Houten, J. (1977). The performance feedback system in the special education classroom: An analysis of public posting and peer comments. *Behavior Therapy*, 8(3), 366–376. https://doi.org/10.1016/S0005-7894(77)80071-3.

Part II

Preparation for Implementation

4 Creating a Positive Environment

Alexandra Hilt-Panahon and Kennedi Alstead

Creating a Positive Environment

Prior to starting any intervention, it is best practice to ensure that you have created a positive environment for all students. Regardless of whether you are in a classroom or therapeutic setting, these suggestions will help to provide a setting that is conducive to successful intervention. By creating an environment where expectations are clear, and reinforcement is provided, you can often prevent additional problematic behaviors for your target students and other students as well. A high level of structure and predictable activities will allow children and adolescents to know what to do and what your expectations are in a given situation.

The effective management of student behavior has long been identified as a critical skill of successful teachers (Kauffman et al., 1991). Research has specified several key indicators of effective management, including positive student-teacher interactions, positive feedback, clear rules and expectations, and consistent response to student behavior. Unfortunately, research in classrooms indicates these features are not always in place (Chaffee et al., 2017.) It is disheartening to know that research shows that teachers often do not provide praise to students for appropriate behaviors consistently, while using negative consequences regularly (Sutherland et al., 2000). This occurs, despite the fact that we know punitive consequences are not the most ethical or moral ways to address problem behaviors in classrooms (DiGennaro Reed, & Lovett, 2008). The low rates of reinforcement for appropriate behavior and high rates of negative interactions offer an explanation for ongoing behavior problems in classrooms.

In this chapter, a variety of ways to create and maintain a positive environment in whatever setting you are working will be provided. Each may be addressed individually, or all at once depending on the needs of your children and the environment.

Reinforcement and Punishment

The first step in creating a predictable environment is the amount of reinforcement available to students in the group, as well as how much and in what

DOI: 10.4324/9781003128663-6

Table 4.1 Reinforcement and Punishment

	You like it	**You don't like it**
I give it to you	Positive Reinforcement	Positive Punishment
I take it away	Negative Punishment	Negative Reinforcement

form punishment is provided. Reinforcement is, by definition, anything that increases the likelihood that a behavior will occur again in the future. Punishment is anything that decreases the likelihood that a behavior will occur again (Arzin & Holtz, 1966). Both can work together to help students learn appropriate behaviors.

When a specific behavior is followed by a favorable outcome that behavior will be more likely to happen in the future. Reinforcement and punishment can take one of two forms, positive or negative. In this context, positive refers to the addition of something into the environment. Negative refers to the removal of stimuli from the environment. Reinforcement refers to things that will increase behavior and punishment will decrease it. The following graphic provides a simple description.

Positive Reinforcement. As we can see in the diagram above, the effect of the consequence will be influenced by the value of the outcome. Positive reinforcement is when something is added to the environment that makes a behavior more likely to occur, while negative reinforcement is when something is removed from the environment that makes a behavior more likely to occur. So, if there is something you like and I give it to you contingent on your behavior, you will be more likely to engage in that behavior again in the future. For example, if you love candy and I give you a piece of candy every time you answer a question in class, you will be more likely to answer future questions because you know that you will receive a piece of candy. In this example, the candy acts as a reinforcer. Getting candy after answering questions makes you more likely to answer questions in the future.

Negative Reinforcement. Another way to increase a desired behavior, is to remove unwanted stimulus from a person's environment. Negative reinforcement is one of the most misunderstood ways to change behavior. As stated earlier, reinforcement always increases the likelihood a behavior will occur again in the future. Negative reinforcement is often confused with punishment, but it actually does increase behavior by removing an unwanted stimulus. A great example of negative reinforcement is your car seatbelt alarm. The alarm begins to chime as soon as you turn your car on, and does not stop until you buckle your seatbelt. As soon as you put the seatbelt on (the desired behavior), the alarm (unwanted stimulus) stops. This makes it more likely that you will keep your seatbelt on and put it on the next time you get in the car.

Positive Punishment. The term positive punishment sounds like an oxymoron, but we must remember that the "positive" refers to the addition of something in the environment. So, if I give you something that you do not want, you are less likely to repeat that behavior in order to avoid the unwanted consequence. So, for example, if a teacher gives students chocolate every time they answer a question, she will likely think that she is reinforcing the students. While the chocolate would serve as a reinforcer for students who want the chocolate, it may serve as a punisher for some. If a child in the class does not like chocolate, being given some after answering a question will not lead to the student being motivated to answer questions in the future. The value of the consequence will be important to determine prior to using any consequence. We often end up reinforcing unwanted behaviors and punishing the desired simply by choosing the wrong consequences.

Negative Punishment. Finally, negative punishment is when something desired is taken away in order to decrease the likelihood that a behavior will occur again in the future. Anyone who has ever been grounded as a child understands this concept. Something you like (going out with friends) is taken away (negative) when you do something you aren't supposed to do (talk back to our parents). This will make you think twice about talking back the next time the situation arises.

When designing a positive environment, it is important to remember that you do not need to choose from one of these options for how to respond to behaviors. In fact, reinforcement and punishment work together to help people learn what is expected and what is unacceptable in a given situation. By incorporating both reinforcement and punishment into your structured plan you will increase the likelihood of a well-run classroom/ therapeutic setting.

There are several guidelines to consider when first implementing planned reinforcement into an environment. Reinforcement occurs whether we plan for it or not, so it is important to closely look at the environment that you have created and determine if you are, in fact, reinforcing the behaviors you want to see from your students/clients. The following are some scenarios that may help to exemplify just how easy it is to unintentionally reinforce the wrong behavior. Read each of the following scenarios and consider which behaviors are likely to happen again in the future and why.

Scenario 1: After a 20-minute large group math lesson, Mrs. Washington tells her students that they will have 20 minutes to work quietly at their desks on a worksheet practicing the skills just discussed in the lesson. Johnny, who has struggled throughout the school year with math, looks at the worksheet and realizes he has no idea how to do the work. While the other students in the class get started on their work, Johnny throws his worksheet to the floor and puts his head on the desk. Mrs. Washington goes to Johnny and asks him to pick it up. When he refuses, Johnny is sent to the office for the remainder of the class period. This occurs every day until the end of the semester.

Scenario 2: A father and his toddler are at the grocery store doing the family's weekly shopping. The little girl sees a candy bar at the checkout line and asks her father nicely if she may have one. Her father says no, she does not need a candy bar. As soon as Dad says no, the little girl starts crying loudly. Dad tells her to stop, which makes her fall to the floor, kick her feet and yell even more loudly. At this point, people in the store are starting to stare. Dad picks up the child, tells her to pick a candy bar, and after paying leaves the store.

Scenario 3: A baby is playing on the floor while his mother is reading a book. She looks up and sees that the baby has the TV remote in his mouth. Mom says "don't eat that!" and takes the remote away from the baby. As soon as she does, the baby starts crying. Mom tries to continue reading her book, but the baby just keeps getting louder. Finally, Mom gives up and hands the remote back to the little boy. He immediately starts sucking on the remote and Mom is able to read again in peace.

In each of these scenarios, unwanted behavior is unintentionally being reinforced. While the adults in these scenarios are trying to stop the children from behaving "badly," they are in fact actually making it more likely that the student will engage in that behavior again in the future. Looking at the first example, the student is acting out in the classroom so the teacher sent him to the office. This happens every day in all types of classrooms around the nation. The teacher believes that she is punishing the boy for his inappropriate behavior. But if we look at the definition of punishment, it is something that will likely decrease the behavior in the future. Given that the student didn't understand the assignment and did not want to do it, sending him to the office for the rest of the period was actually welcomed by the student. Instead of punishing him, the teacher has actually given him exactly what he wanted. He did not have to do the assignment he didn't know how to do. So, what happened in this situation? To answer that questions we can take a look at the Antecedent-Behavior-Consequence chain:

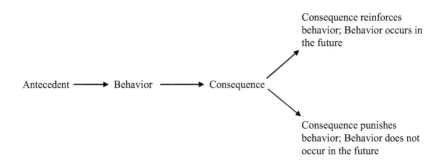

Figure 4.1 ABC

If we apply this to Scenario 1, it looks as follows:

Figure 4.2

So, despite the fact that the teacher was trying to make the student stop his bad behavior, she instead provided an outcome that was desirable for him. This will make him more likely to do the same the next time he is faced with work that he cannot complete. The teacher is also more likely to send him out of the room when he acts out, because this will remove the unwanted behavior from the classroom.

In scenario 1, it should be noted that the teacher is also negatively reinforced by the student's removal. It is easy to become trapped in a cycle of reinforcing inappropriate behaviors in order to escape aversive situations. Removing the student gives the student what he wanted (not to have to do the work), and also gives the teacher what she wanted (no longer having to deal with a tantrum). This situation is known as the "negative reinforcement trap." We may inadvertently reinforce a student for unwanted behavior without even realizing it because we are simultaneously reinforced by the removal of the aversive situation. It is important to recognize if the consequences you provide are actually improving student behavior, or if they just temporarily reduce the problematic behavior.

Heitzman (1983) proposed guidelines for the use of punishment in educational settings that are still relevant today.

First, it is recommended that whatever consequence is used, it is important to make sure that it is in fact punishing. As discussed above, if a student wants to leave class, sending them to the principal's office will likely serve to reinforce the behavior that was supposed to be punished.

Next, it is important to make sure that no "unauthorized escape" from punishment is allowed (Heitzman, 1983). In other words, if punishment is used, it must be implemented with 100% integrity. For example, if a teacher tells a student that they will not be able to go out to recess unless are aggressive to other students in the class, the removal of recess is meant to serve as a punishment to decrease aggressive behavior. On the surface, this seems like it would be effective in reducing the aggressive behavior is the student likes recess. If, however, the teacher has said that all week and every day the student goes out to recess anyway, even when they are aggressive, then the punishment will not be effective. The student knows that there will not be follow through on the consequence and therefore it does not decrease the aggressive behavior.

Research has also shown that for it to be effective, punishment should be only as severe as needed to decrease behavior. It is important to remember that punishment does not need to be harmful to a person in order to be effective. We should never look to implement consequences that are hurtful, demeaning, or ostracizing for anyone.

Punishment should also be immediate and consistent. In order for a consequence to act as a punisher, the individual must associate that consequence with the undesired behavior. In order to make that association effectively and efficiently the consequence should follow the target behavior as soon as it occurs. The more immediate the consequence the stronger the association will be. In addition, the more consistently the consequence is applied (ideally every time the behavior occurs) the association is strengthened and the punishment is more likely to be effective.

An excellent example of the principals outlined above that occurs in everyday life is speeding tickets. Speeding tickets are a form of positive punishment that is meant to reduce the likelihood that a person will speed again in the future. While tickets are considered a punishment, it is important to look at the factors that may impact how effective this consequence is at reducing speeding. First, we need to look at whether or not the consequence will actually serve as a punishment. Given that tickets typically run in the hundreds of dollars it is likely that this would be a deterrent for most people. Next, we need to look at "unauthorized escapes". Is it possible to get out of a speeding ticket? In reality there are a variety of ways to not have to pay a speeding ticket, so to some extent unauthorized escapes are possible. This will weaken the effectiveness of the punishment. Finally, when we look at the immediacy and consistency of the application of the punishment. Does everyone who speeds get a ticket every time? Are they immediately pulled over and made to pay the fine on the spot. In most situations, this is not the case. Many people speed regularly and are never pulled over or given a ticket. People know that there is a risk to speeding because you may get a ticket, but the reality of the situation is that it is unlikely that you will be caught and less likely that you will receive a punishing consequence. This explains why many drivers still speed even through there is a punishment for doing it.

Rules and Expectations

Another important factor to consider when establishing a positive environment is to determine the rules and/or expectations you will have for the group. This can be done in one of two ways. You can decide on rules and expectations yourself and share them with students, or you can ask the members of the group to participate in the development of expectations. There are benefits and drawbacks to both. By creating the rules on your own, you have complete control over the expectations. You have the ability to target the specific behaviors that you want to address and can tailor to the needs of the students with whom you work. By allowing students the opportunity to help create the expectations, it provides them with a sense of ownership and may increase compliance. If you choose to have student involvement in development, it is important to be sure to determine ahead of time what expectations are non-negotiable for you. These should be included along with whatever students contribute.

Regardless of how you decide to develop the setting expectations, there are several things to keep in mind. Best practice dictates that the following guidelines be followed when developing rules. First, when developing the expectations, it is important not to have too many. Research suggests that three to five expectations are ideal. This allows for students to remember them, and makes it easier to keep track of student compliance.

Rules should be positively stated, letting the students know what they should do, not just what not to do. For example, instead of saying "No running," the rule "walk" should be used. No running tells the student what not to do to avoid punishment, but it gives no guidance for what he or she should do to meet expectations. If the rule is "No running," would skipping down the hall be acceptable? While we can infer the intention for this rule is for students to walk, a clearly stated expectation takes away all ambiguity and makes it easier to enforce.

The expectations that you create should be written in a way that is observable and measurable. If we cannot see it or count it, we cannot track it and make sure that students are following the rules. For example, we often see rules like "Pay attention." While attending is an important skill in the classroom or therapeutic setting, it is an internal behavior and therefore cannot be observed. If I cannot see you engage in a behavior, I cannot provide feedback and/or reinforcement for that behavior. As such, defining behaviors in an observable way is vital to the success for reinforcement-based programs. While we cannot see a student paying attention, there are behaviors that help us determine if in fact they have been attentive to the lesson. For example, we can see a student sitting in his or her chair and facing the teacher. We can also see a student following directions and we can see a student's work after it has been completed. So, expectations like "eyes on teacher" or "follow directions" will make it easy to track and reward good behavior.

Routines and Procedures

In addition to specific rules and expectations, it is also important to provide children with predictable routines and procedures for the environment, whether it is in the classroom or in a therapeutic setting. Students should be actively taught the procedures for the setting including how to enter the space, what to do when they get there, and any other routines that will ensure that things run smoothly.

Organization of Physical Space

Another consideration is how the setting is organized. You should examine the way in which furniture, tables, cabinets, etc. are arranged in the space. Does it provide for easy movement around the room? Do children have ample room to spread out? Are there specific areas of the classroom or other setting that are devoted to specific activities that typically occur (independent work, group time, breaks, etc.). The environment should be organized in a way that will promote positive behaviors in children. This will decrease the amount of inappropriate behavior as well as allow for students to engage in positive behaviors. (Sprick et al., 2021). The organization of the environment also allows for more active interaction and monitoring from the adults in the classroom which can also reduce problem behaviors. When setting up the classroom, consider how the arrangement of the room will allow for positive interactions among those on the room while also maintaining order. Carefully arranging the setting prior to the start of school can have a huge impact on the behaviors once classes begin.

Use of Effective Teaching Strategies

Another area in which students may struggle is academics. While there are many factors that contribute to academic deficits, one important hypothesized variable, with some empirical support is the limited instruction provided by teachers (e.g., Wehby et al., 2003). Increasing student opportunities to engage in academic activities is unmistakably essential. At the same time, it is imperative that students are instructed at the appropriate level. Instructional match is defined as how closely a student's skills match the difficulty of instructional material (Daly et al., 1996). If there is not a good instructional match, students will not fully benefit from instruction.

Numerous studies have documented the relationship between the level of task difficulty and both off-task and disruptive behaviors (Cooper et al., 1992; Gunter et al., 1993). For example, Meyer (1999) conducted functional analyses with four students exhibiting off-task behavior. Analyses revealed that high rates of problem behavior were associated with difficult work for three of four participants. Intervention that addressed difficulty (help provided on request) served to reduce off-task behavior for all three students. Collectively, this body of research highlights the importance of matching work difficulty to each student's instructional level. Further, the research suggests collateral improvements on academic performance and reductions in problem behavior, in addition to increases in on-task behavior.

Although research has shown that teachers can judge whether students are performing at grade level with moderate to high levels of accuracy (McKevett & Kiss, 2019;), recent studies indicate teachers' judgments related to a student's specific instructional level are not accurate (Krämer & Zimmermann, 2021). Fortunately, instructional level can be easily and objectively established through survey level assessment. This approach provides teachers with a simple, time efficient method of assessing student skills and requires minimal training or expertise in assessment (Shapiro, 2004).

Once instructional level has been established, the amount of opportunities to respond (OTR) provided to students should be addressed. This approach has been demonstrated to be effective in classrooms and appears to be a pivotal intervention in that collateral benefits include increased correct responding and decreased problem behavior.

In a review of the use of OTR with students with EBD, Sutherland and Wehby (2001) identified six studies, each of which demonstrated increases in task engagement, along with other collateral effects. A study by Sutherland et al. (2003) demonstrated the applicability and effectiveness of this intervention implemented class-wide. Procedures included teacher prediction of his baseline rate of OTR/minute, feedback about observed baseline rate, description of benefits of increase OTR rate, goal setting, ongoing feedback, and self-graphing. Direct observations indicated increases in task engagement and correct responses per minute and decreases in disruptive behaviors class-wide. This study illustrates the applicability and effectiveness of the procedure when implemented class-wide with students with EBD. Further, it appears that the intervention is relatively easy for teachers to implement with fidelity (Sutherland & Wehby, 2001).

Interactions between students, staff, and teachers

It is important to remember that the social interactions that children witness can also have an impact on their behavior. Good models of appropriate social skills provide students with an example that they can learn from and copy in the future. As such, it is important that the adults in the environment demonstrate the behaviors that are expected from the students. Observe your own and other adult behaviors to ensure that all are speaking respectfully to each other and the children, using manners as expected in the setting, and refraining from negative interactions as much as possible. By creating a positive environment where the expectations for everyone's behavior is consistent, you are creating a situation in which children will be more likely to be successful.

Social Skills instruction

One thing that is important to remember before starting tootling is that the students need to be able to perform prosocial behaviors in order for peers to see and report them. So, it is very important that students have these skills before we have an expectation of them to use them. Social skills instruction is an effective way to teach these skills to students that are lacking. For a more thorough discussion of social skills interventions and their effectiveness, please see Chapter 5 of this book.

References

Azrin, N. H., & Holz, W. C. (1966). Punishment. In W. K. Honig (ed.), *Operant Behavior: Areas of Research and Application* (pp. 213–270). Appleton-Century-Crofts.

K. Chaffee, R. K., Briesch, A. M., Johnson, A. H., & Volpe, R. J. (2017). A meta-analysis of class-wide interventions for supporting student behavior. *School Psychology Review*, 46(2), 149–164.

Cooper, L. J., Wacker, D. P., Thursby, D., Plagmann, L. A., Harding, J., Millard, T., & Derby M. (1992). Analysis of the effects of task preferences, task demands, and adult attention on child behavior in outpatient and classroom settings. *Journal of Applied Behavior Analysis*, 25(4), 823–840. https://doi.org/10.1901/jaba.1992.25-823.

Daly III, E. J., Martens, B. K., Kilmer A., Massie, D. R. (1996). The effects of instructional match and content overlap on generalized reading performance. *Journal of Applied Behavior Analysis*, 29(4), 507–518. https://doi.org/10.1901/jaba.1996.29-507.

DiGennaro Reed, F. D., & Lovett, B. J. (2008). Views on the efficacy and ethics of punishment: Results from a national survey. *International Journal of Behavioral and Consultation Therapy*, 4(1), 61–67. https://doi.org/10.1037/h0100832.

Gunter, P. L., Denny, R. K., Jack, S. L., Shores, R. E., & Nelson, C. M. (1993). Aversive stimuli in academic interactions between students with serious emotional disturbance and their teachers. *Behavioral Disorders*, 18(4), 265–274. https://doi.org/10.1177/019874299301800405.

Heitzman, A. J. (1983). Discipline and the use of punishment. *Education*, 104(1), 17–22.

Kauffman, J. M., Wong, K. L. H., Lloyd, J. W., Hung, L. Y., & Pullen, P. L. (1991). What puts pupils at risk? An analysis of classroom teachers' judgments of pupils' behavior. *Remedial and Special Education*, 12(5), 7–16. https://doi.org/10.1177/074193259101200503.

Krämer, S., & Zimmermann, F. (2021). Students with emotional and behavioral disorder and teachers' stereotypes – Effects on teacher judgments. *The Journal of Experimental Education*. https://doi.org/10.1080/00220973.2021.1934809.

McKevett, N. M., & Kiss, A. J. (2019). The influence of data on teachers' judgments of students' early reading and math skills. *Psychology in the Schools*, 56(7), 1157–1172. https://doi.org/10.1002/pits.22256.

Meyer, K. A. (1999). Functional analysis and treatment of problem behavior exhibited by elementary school children. *Journal of Applied Behavior Analysis*, 32(2), 229–232. https://doi.org/10.1901/jaba.1999.32-229.

Shapiro, E. S. (2004). *Academic skills problems: Direct assessment and intervention* (3rd ed.). Guilford Press. https://www.proquest.com/books/academic-skills-problems-third-edition-direct/docview/62082137/se-2?accountid=12259.

Sprick, J., Sprick, R., Edwards, J., & Coughlin, C. (2021). *CHAMPS: A proactive & positive approach to classroom management* (3rd ed.). Ancora. https://ancorapublishing.com/product/champs-third-edition/.

Sutherland, K. S., Alder, N., & Gunter, P. L. (2003). The effects of varying rates of opportunities to respond to academic requests on the classroom behavior of students with EBD. *Journal of Emotional and Behavioral Disorders*, 11(4), 239–248. https://doi.org/10.1177/10634266030110040501.

Sutherland, K. S., & Wehby, J. H. (2001). Exploring the relationship between increased opportunities to respond to academic requests and the academic and behavioral outcomes of students with EBD: A review. *Remedial and Special Education*, 22(2), 113–121. https://doi.org/10.1177/074193250102200205.

Sutherland, K. S., Wehby, J. H., & Copeland, S. R. (2000). Effect of varying rates of behavior-specific praise on the on-task behavior of students with EBD. *Journal of Emotional and Behavioral Disorders*, 8(1), 2–8. https://doi.org/10.1177/106342660000800101.

Wehby, J. H., Lane, K. L., & Falk, K. B. (2003). Academic instruction for students with emotional and behavioral disorders. *Journal of Emotional and Behavioral Disorders*, 11(4), 194–197. https://doi.org/10.1177/10634266030110040101.

5   Social Skills Interventions

Alexandra Hilt-Panahon and Kennedi Alstead

Social Skills Interventions

Prior to starting a tootling program, or any reinforcement-based intervention, it is imperative that the students participating in the intervention have the skills necessary to be successful. Reinforcement based programs are designed to encourage the practice of skills with the intent of building fluency. In order for practice to be effective, a person must already have the skill in their behavioral repertoire. Specifically, if a child has not yet learned how to perform a behavior, they will not be able to practice it. If a person is asked to practice a skill they have not learned, they will likely practice errors and it will be difficult for them to gain mastery of that skill. In order to avoid this situation, it is important to ascertain a child's ability to perform any skill before asking them to engage in practice. This holds true for social skills as with any other skill. Before we can begin a reinforcement-based program, designed to encourage practice, we must ensure that students are able to independently perform the skills they are required to perform in order to gain access to reinforcement. If it is found that a child does not know how to perform the skill in question, no amount of reinforcement will entice them to do it. As an example, consider the following scenario:

> Mrs. Johnson wants all of the students to know their times tables. She tells them that they will be learning the times tables over the course of several days. On Monday, she shows the students all of the times tables. She then tells them that she will give them a test at the end of the class and any student that gets 100% correct will earn a prize. After one week Mrs. Johnson can't understand why her students aren't getting any better at the problems. They practice answering them every day and she has offered a prize if they do well, but most of the students are getting most of the problems wrong each day.

In this scenario, there are multiple reasons why Mrs. Johnson's class isn't getting better at their times tables. First, Mrs. Johnson never actually taught the students how to answer the problems, she just showed them the answers.

DOI: 10.4324/9781003128663-7

This means that students are likely relying on their memory to answer, rather than having the skill to actually solve the problem. Second, the students are being given time to practice, but since they don't know how to solve the problem, they are likely answering problems incorrectly. If they repeatedly practice errors, it will be more difficult for them to learn how to answer the problems correctly. Lastly, the incentive of a prize if students answer correctly is completely ineffective given that the students don't know how to answer correctly. No amount of incentive will magically give the students the answers to the questions. If they don't know how to solve the problem, nothing will entice them to accurately answer the question.

This example highlights the importance of knowing how to perform a skill before being asked to do it independently. It makes sense that a student would not know how to solve a math problem until they learn how to do it. Similarly, if you were offered $1 million to read a book written in Spanish, you would not be able to earn that money unless you know how to read Spanish. No amount of money (i.e., reinforcement) will entice you to suddenly know how to read the book. The same is true for children learning new skills.

The mechanisms related to learning a skill operate differently than those related to practicing a skill already learned. As such, how we promote these actions should be different as well. While this seems fairly obvious related to learning new academic skills, we often forget that people need to learn social skills and behaviors in a similar way. Because the process of learning how to interact with others often occurs in more natural environments without formal teaching, we sometimes forget that these skills are learned.

The relationships students have with their peers while in school are key to their school experience. Research has shown that early prosocial behavior with peers strongly predicts the level of academic achievement. In addition, students with higher levels of prosocial behavior tend to become more preferred adults (Slee & Rigby, 1993). The interactions children have with others are essential to forming friendships and connections to school. When students struggle to form positive peer relationships, they can be socially withdrawn or choose negative ways to achieve peer interactions (Wentzel, 2017). These friendship relationships can help students to process how and what they learn in the school environment.

In order to address these concerns, it is important that social skills are actively addressed as part of the curriculum. Direct teaching of socially appropriate behaviors, particularly at the younger grades, can significantly reduce the need for intervention later on. In this chapter we will provide an overview of some of the most popular and well researched approaches to teaching social skills in schools. This is by no means an exhaustive list. It will, however, provide professionals with a list of tried-and-true methods as a place to start.

Published Social Skills Intervention Packages

Given the need in schools for practical ways of teaching social skills to students, a variety of Social, Emotional, Learning (SEL) curricula and interventions have been published over the last several years. The benefits of using a published intervention is that there is typically research to support its use. This takes the guesswork out of identifying an effective intervention. It is important to review the evidence base, however, even with such interventions. While most have the data to support their use, some are published without research that demonstrates efficacy.

The Second Step is one such SEL curriculum which emphasizes directly teaching students skills which will help strengthen the students' ability to learn, manage their emotions, have empathy for others, and increase their ability to solve problems. Multiple research studies have shown the effects of Second Step on students' social emotional competence and reduction of antisocial behaviors, in particular physical aggression (Frey et al., 2005). Each of the Second Step lessons contain the following components to help teach students appropriate social skills: the SEL warm up and review activity from the previous lesson, a short story or film followed by a discussion, skills practice and then a wrap up in which the lesson for the day is summarized. The Second Step has a logic model which says that when students are provided direct instruction in social–emotional skills and they are given the opportunities to practice those skills, as well as receive reinforcement for demonstrating the skills, they are more likely to show improvement. The Second Step is the most widely used SEL curriculum in schools (Low et al., 2015). Numerous studies have shown that students receiving the implementation of Second Step lessons had an increase and showed improvement in their social skills when compared to children in control classrooms, based on teacher reports (Frey et al., 2000). One of the reasons this curriculum is so beneficial is because it gives the students who are receiving the intervention a step by step, orderly process to work through problems as well as giving them replacement behaviors and an opportunity to role play and practice their strategies.

Video Modeling

One strategy that has been used to teach a range of skills for children, particularly those with ASD, is video modeling (VM). Video modeling is a widely used evidenced based practice for dealing with challenging behaviors, particularly for individuals with Autism. Video modeling is a way of teaching that uses a video recording to show a visual model of the targeted behavior or skill. Basic video modeling involves recording someone that is not the target learner engaging in the target behavior or skill (i.e., models). The target learner then views the video at a later time. In the studies that serve as the foundation for the evidence base, video modeling was implemented in both school and home settings (Franzone & Collet-Klingenberg, 2008). In the evidence-based studies, the domains of communication, social, academic/cognition, and play were represented and with children ranging from early childhood to middle school (Franzone & Collet-Klingenberg, 2008).

Social Stories

A social story is made up of descriptions of social and behavioral cues that an individual student can be taught, directive statements that tell a student how they are supposed to act or respond to a cue, statements describing the thoughts or feelings of others during interactions, and descriptions of the settings in order to help the student gain context of the social story (Gray, 1998). Social stories have become a common way for teachers to introduce specific skills for students to improve behaviors in the classroom or home environments. Often, social stories are used in order to teach a replacement behavior for a negative behavior such as talking out in class, vocalizing, or aggressive behaviors toward peers or teachers. Social stories are also a way to teach students social skills. By incorporating a social story into the daily routine of a student, teachers are able to incorporate the use of task analysis, visual aids, social modeling and corrective feedback in order to improve social skills (Schneider, & Goldstein, 2010).

A study by Delano and Snell (2006) found that each participant demonstrated an increase in the duration of time they were socially engaged with their training peer, as well as a novel peer in the classroom. The social stories increased positive behaviors in all participants. Moudry Quilty (2007) conducted a study to teach paraprofessionals how to write and implement social stories. Each paraprofessional developed a social story specific to the individual needs of the student they supported in the classroom setting. The implementation of the social story intervention demonstrated that when implemented with fidelity, the students were able to demonstrate positive behavior changes. Those changes were not only seen during the intervention phase, but during maintenance six and nine weeks after the intervention phase.

Litras et al. (2010) used video modeling in combination with social stories in order to help participants improve the skills being addressed. The participants in the study demonstrated an increase in their positive interactions across all three skills (greeting, inviting, and responding). The students were able to maintain these skills in follow up observations. There were other studies that looked at using social stories as an intervention to support students who do not have ASD or related disorders. Schneider and Goldstein (2009) looked at using social stories for students with language impairment. The students all have some form of speech or language impairment, and struggled with appropriate social behaviors in the classroom setting. On-task and off-task behaviors were identified for each student and a social story was created to address each student's particular behavior challenges. All of the participants demonstrated an increase in on-task behaviors both during intervention and later observed during maintenance.

Social Narratives

In previous research, social narratives have been successfully utilized as an intervention to teach a target behavior and offer examples of appropriate responding. Social narratives can be individualized to include the details of the situation-appropriate responses and describe the thoughts and feelings of other people involved. This is beneficial because individuals with ASD can have difficulty using and understanding eye contact, facial expressions, body language, tones of voice, initiating interactions, responding to others, maintaining interactions, and interpreting the thoughts and feelings of others (Golzari et al., 2015). Social narratives can be easily implemented effectively with little training (Crozier & Tincani, 2005). This is important because it means that social narratives can be easily utilized in classrooms, by multiples staff, require little training, individualized to the participant and situation, and are cost effective. Social narratives target expanding participants' social skills in the area of interacting with peers. Examples of possible targets include playing with an adult facilitated turn taking game for at least three turns, initiating or joining a play scheme with words, gestures, or voice output devices; imitating play of other peers, and parallel play by sharing a common base toy and materials with a peer for at least five minutes. Using a social narrative to increase these behaviors has shown success in previous research because it is an approach that can be used to establish rules and routines social situations that can be an area of difficulty for individuals with ASD (Sansosti & Powell-Smith, 2006).

Positive Peer Reporting

Positive Peer Reporting (PPR) is an intervention to improve the social interactions and social status of socially rejected or withdrawn youth. It is a class wide intervention with the main focus on target students who are socially rejected or withdrawn. PPR encourages students to notice positive interactions and report on those interactions. In essence, ignoring the inappropriate behaviors. These reports are made daily during a specific time of day. Each student is provided an opportunity to report a positive interaction with a target student. These reports are tracked for a class wide reward. The target students receive the positive report, which helps them to fell connected to the class. It increases their level of prosocial behaviors and increases the amount of interactions with their peers. It creates a more positive classroom environment. Children often respond well to interventions that emphasize, identify and counter negative emotions and thoughts, such as Positive Peer Reporting.

Ervin et al. (1996) was one of the first studies completed using PPR in a residential setting. PPR intervention improved the prosocial interactions and decreased the negative interactions with this student. During withdrawal phases, her negative behavior increased, and prosocial involvement decreased. The data suggests the PPR intervention was beneficial in changing the negative behaviors and increasing the positive interactions among his peers.

Now more than ever, appropriate social and behavioral development are at the forefront of necessary skills needed for students as they enter Kindergarten and beyond. For children already at risk, the continued occurrence of problem behaviors can be detrimental for their future. (Benedict et al., 2007). By addressing these behaviors early with direct, specific instruction, it is possible to improve student behavior and provide a path for success that would not otherwise be possible. Addressing social skills in the classroom allows teachers to ensure that students have the skills necessary to be successful both in the classroom as well as in other environments such as home and the community at large. Ensuring knowledge of social skills also has the potential to eliminate the need for more targeted interventions. For all of these reasons, it is recommended that educators evaluate the level of proficiency of students' social skills and provide any necessary instruction prior to starting a performance based intervention program such as tooling.

References

Benedict, E. A., Horner, R. H., & Squires, J. K. (2007). Assessment and implementation of positive behavior support in preschools. *Topics in Early Childhood Special Education*, 27(3), 174–192. https://doi.org/10.1177/02711214070270030801.

Crozier, S., & Tincani, M. J. (2005). Using a modified social story to decrease disruptive behavior of a child with autism. *Focus on Autism and Other Developmental Disabilities*, 20(3), 150–157. https://doi.org/10.1177/10883576050200030301.

Delano, M., & Snell, M. E. (2006). The effects of social stories on the social engagement of children with autism. *Journal of Positive Behavior Interventions*, 8(1), 29–42. https://doi.org/10.1177/10983007060080010501.

Ervin, R. A., Miller, P. M., & Friman, P. C. (1996). Feed the hungry bee: Using positive peer reports to improve the social interactions and acceptance of a socially rejected girl in residential care. *Journal of Applied Behavior Analysis*, 29(2), 251–253. https://doi.org/10.1901/jaba.1996.29-251.

Franzone, E., & Collet-Klingenberg, L. (2008). Overview of video modeling. National Professional Development Center on Autism Spectrum Disorders. https://csesa.fpg. unc.edu/sites/csesa.fpg.unc.edu/files/ebpbriefs/VideoModeling_Overview_1.pdf.

Frey, K. S., Hirschstein, M. K., & Guzzo, B. A. (2000). Second step: Preventing aggression by promoting social competence. *Journal of Emotional and Behavioral Disorders*, 8(2), 102–112. https://doi.org/10.1177/106342660000800206.

Frey, K. S., Nolen, S. B., Edstrom, L. V. S., & Hirschstein, M. K. (2005). Effects of a school-based social–emotional competence program: Linking children's goals, attributions, and behavior. *Journal of applied developmental psychology*, 26(2), 171–200.

Golzari, F., Hemati Alamdarloo, G., & Moradi, S. (2015). The effect of a social stories intervention of the social skills of male students with autism spectrum disorder. *SAGE Open*, 5(4), 1–8. https://doi.org/10.1177/2158244015621599.

Gray, C. A. (1998). Social stories and comic strip conversations with students with Asperger syndrome and high-functioning autism. In E. Schopler, G. B. Mesibov, & L. J. Kunce (Eds.), *Asperger syndrome or high-functioning autism*. (1st ed., pp. 167–198). https://doi.org/10.1007/978-1-4615-5369-4.

Litras, S., Moore, D. W., & Anderson, A. (2010). Using video self-modelled social stories to teach social skills to a young child with autism. *Autism Research and Treatment, 2010*, 1–9. https://doi.org/10.1155/2010/834979.

Low, S., Cook, C. R., Smolkowski, K., & Buntain-Ricklefs, J. (2015). Promoting social-emotional competence: An evaluation of the elementary version of second step. *Journal of School Psychology*, 53(6), 463–477, https://doi.org/10.1016/j.jsp.2015.09.002.

Moudry Quilty, K. (2007). Teaching paraprofessionals how to write and implement social stories for students with autism spectrum disorders. *Remedial and Special Education*, 28(3), 182–189. https://doi.org/10.1177/07419325070280030701.

Slee, P. T., & Rigby, K. (1993). Australian school children's self appraisal of interpersonal relations: The bullying experience. *Child psychiatry and human development*, 23(4), 273–282.

Sansosti, F. J., & Powell-Smith, K. A. (2006). Using social stories to improve the social behavior of children with Asperger syndrome. *Journal of Positive Behavior Interventions*, 8(1), 43–57. https://doi.org/10.1177/10983007060080010601.

Schneider, N., & Goldstein, H. (2009). Social Stories improve the on-task behavior of children with language impairment. *Journal of Early Intervention*, 31(3), 250–264. https://doi.org/10.1177/1053815109339564.

Schneider, N., & Goldstein, H. (2010). Using social stories and visual schedules to improve socially appropriate behaviors in children with autism. *Journal of Positive Behavior Interventions*, 12(3), 149–160. https://doi.org/10.1177/1098300709334198.

Wentzel, K. R. (2017). Peer relationships, motivation, and academic performance at school. In A. J. Elliot, C. S. Dweck, & D. S. Yeager (Eds.), *Handbook of competence and motivation: Theory and application* (pp. 586–603). The Guilford Press.

6 How to Implement Tootling

Alexandra Hilt-Panahon and Kennedi Alstead

How to Implement Tootling

Once you have created a positive environment for all children, you can then begin to implement the tootling intervention. This chapter will walk you through the steps necessary for a successful implementation that will lead to positive results for the children with whom you work. We will describe in detail the steps in preparing materials, training children, preparing the staff and other stakeholders. We will conclude with a description of how to conduct the intervention.

Materials

To set up a tootling intervention, first you will need to create the necessary materials. The basic supplies you will need are outlined below. Here we have provided the basic item as well as some possible variations that can be used depending on your particular situation.

Tootle Cards.

First, you will need to determine how students will record their tootles. Tootles should be collected in a way that will provide some form of permanent product. Typically, students are given "tootle cards" where they can write down the positive

Table 6.1 Tootling Card

| WHO: _____ |
| DID WHAT: _____ |
| FOR WHOM: _____ |
| REPORTED BY: _____ |

DOI: 10.4324/9781003128663-8

behaviors of their peers. Typical tootle cards have space for students to write their tootle without any prompts (Cashwell et al., 2001; Cihak et al., 2009; Lambert et al., 2015; Lum et al., 2017).

Tootle cards can be adapted to meet the needs of a variety of students. Variations of tootle cards are discussed in more detail in later chapters of this book.

Tootle Box

Students will need a place to turn in the tootles that they write about their peers. A tootle box is a place where students can submit their tootles. It should be centrally located in the classroom so that all students can see and access it. Ideally, the tootle box should be clear so that students can see approximately how many tootles are in the box at any given time. There are many options for what to use for a tootle box. For example, a large, clear container labeled *Tootles* could be placed on the teacher's desk in the classroom.

Public Posting of Tootle Count

An important aspect of tootling is the group effort needed to meet class-wide goals. In order to assist students in knowing how they are progressing toward their goal, some form of public posting is needed within the classroom. This public posting can take many forms, as long as all students have the ability to understand how many tootles have been completed and how close they are to their goal. One example used in previous research is to use a dry erase poster with an image of a thermometer displayed in the front of the classroom during tootling to provide feedback to the students regarding the daily number of tootles reported by the class. After the teacher reviews the daily tootles, he or she then colors in the number of tootles completed by the class. This provides a visual display for all students to see how many tootles have been completed and how close they are to meeting their goal. Other specific examples and modifications of public posting will be discussed in greater detail in Chapter 7.

Rewards

As discussed in Chapter 3, one of the main components of the tootling intervention is the reinforcement provided contingent on student participation in the intervention. In order for tootling to be effective, the rewards provided to students must be reinforcing to students. In order to ensure the reinforcing properties of the rewards provided, it is important to determine student preferences prior to the start of intervention.

There are numerous ways to identify potential reinforcers, from asking students what they would like to work for, to conducting a formal preference assessment. What the reward is and how it is selected isn't as important as the impact that reward has on the children's behavior. So, the most critical aspect is ensuring the reward selected is motivating for the children and increases participation. There are also other things to consider when choosing the reward.

- Will one reward be effective for all of the children or will it be more effective to have choices?
- Do you have a budget for the rewards, or is it better to offer choices that don't cost money?
- If you are going to buy rewards, what is your budget and how long can you maintain the purchases?
- If you choose to use activities as a reward, will there be any negative effects from this? Specifically, could the activity lead to problematic behavior? How much instructional/therapeutic time will be lost to the activity?
- Will you allow food to be a possible reward? Will this be problematic for any children in the classroom? It is important to make sure that no one has any food allergies. In addition, some students may have other dietary restrictions that will need to be taken into consideration before offering choices.

Data Collection System

One of the most important things to consider before starting any intervention, including tootling, is how you will determine the effectiveness of the intervention. There is so little time to create positive outcomes for children, it is important to be sure that what we devote time and energy to actually has a positive effect. The best way to do that is to look objectively at the change in behavior from before to after the intervention was implemented. Objective evaluation requires specific, objective data. The complexity of your data collection plan can vary, depending on how precise you need to be. A more formal data collection method may be warranted if formal documentation of behavior change is needed. A complete description of formal data collection can be found in Chapter 11.

Even if formal documentation isn't needed, it is still important to gather data to determine intervention effectiveness. You should first identify what behaviors you are looking to change. The following section describes behaviors that research has shown are positively impacted by tootling and how to define them.

Target Behaviors

On-task Behavior

Research has shown that tootling has a positive impact on students' on-task behavior. Tootling puts a spotlight on positive behaviors in the classroom, and students respond to this positive environment with positive behavior. Tracking students on-task behavior is a good way to evaluate whether or not the intervention is having an impact on students' behavior. Students who are on-task are less likely to be disruptive, making on-task ideal for decision making purposes. On-task behavior should be defined in observable, measurable terms before you begin the intervention. It is vital to ensure that all involved in the intervention have a clear understanding of what is expected of students. This includes all staff members working with the students, as well as the students themselves. For example, one way to define on-task behavior is that a student is on-task if they are engaged (e.g., passively or actively) in an assigned activity. Examples include a student sitting in their seat, following along in a book, answering teacher-asked questions, sitting quietly while the teacher is talking, working independently at their desk, and raising their hand to ask a question. Non-examples include playing with items not related to the task, talking to peers when the student is expected to attend to the teacher or task, or putting their head on the desk.

Disruptive Behavior

Disruptive behavior is another simple way to evaluate the effectiveness of the tootling intervention. If tootling helps to improve student behavior and increase positive interactions, it stands to reason that less disruptive behavior will occur. Disruptive behavior can be defined as a student engaged in any behavior that is distracting to other individuals in the class. Examples include yelling, cursing, throwing objects, non-compliance, and aggression. Non-examples include inaudibly asking a peer for assistance on a task, doodling, daydreaming, and looking out the window or around the room. Additionally, it may be beneficial to select the most commonly observed disruptive behaviors experienced in the classroom (i.e., audibly talking with peers about an unrelated topic or being out of seat at an unexpected time). This way, progress regarding improvements of disruptive behavior can be tailored toward specific target behaviors for each classroom or setting.

Prosocial Behavior

Prosocial behavior is another important behavior to track before, during, and after the intervention is implemented. Prosocial behavior should be defined in a way that supports and reinforces the behaviors that you would like to see in the group. For example, you may define it as students engaging in a positive social interaction with another student. Examples include helping a student with their homework, answering a peer's question, giving another student a compliment, playing with a peer, and working on an assignment together when it was allowed. Non-examples included answering a teacher's question, obeying classroom rules, and giving a teacher a compliment.

Procedures

Training

Prior to the start of the intervention, it is imperative that all individuals involved in the implementation of the tootling intervention should be well trained in all aspects of the intervention. This includes the teacher, paraprofessionals in the classroom, therapists, counselors, or guardians. In this section we outline specific methods for training individuals who have not read this book.

Training for intervention agents should be provided by someone who has familiarity with tootling either through direct experience with the intervention or through extensive reading of the existing research and resources related to the intervention. Training for intervention agents will vary in length, but typically takes approximately 30 to 60 minutes to complete. The trainer should begin by describing what tootling is and how it is implemented. The protocols for student training and intervention sessions should also be shared. It can be very helpful to role play both student training and intervention implementation with individuals who are not familiar with Tootling, in order to provide exposure to the procedures before intervention is implemented.

Baseline

It is important to collect some form of baseline data prior to the start of Tootling. This can be done in a variety of ways, but is necessary for comparison to levels of both positive and inappropriate behaviors after tootling has been put in place. These data can be as simple as tally marks collected by the teacher or another adult to more complicated systems of data collection using systematic data collection methods.

Preparation for Intervention

Student Training

Prior to the implementation of tootling procedures, it is important to ensure that all students (and staff) have a firm understanding of the intervention and how it works. In order to be sure that this is the case, training sessions should be conducted. This should occur before the intervention begins, rather than waiting until after it starts and realizing that children are confused or unsure how to participate. The training sessions can be conducted by the person or people with the most experience with tootling. This may be the classroom teacher, school psychologist, or social worker, to name a few. During the first day of training, students are provided with examples and non-examples of classmates' helping behaviors. Students are then asked to give their own examples of how they help others at home and at school. Tattling and tootling are defined, and students are given examples of tootling (e.g., helping a student pick up their books, loaning a student a pencil, showing a student how to work through a math problem). Students should then verbally provide their own examples. Responses that fit criteria (i.e., who/classmate did what/helpful behavior, and for whom/who they helped) for tootling should be praised, and corrective feedback can be given when students provide examples that do not fit the criteria. Students should be told why their example does not fit the criteria and an appropriate alternative can then be written.

After students are clear as to the behaviors in question, they should then be taught the tootling procedures. The procedures that will be followed will vary depending on the children participating and the setting you are implementing tootling. Be sure to thoroughly describe all aspects of the procedures and check for understanding as needed.

Often, a second day of student training is needed. During this second session, the definition for tootling should be reviewed and students can be reminded that tootling involves only their classmates' prosocial behaviors. A short review of what was discussed in the session should occur as well. Below is an example of a protocol for a two-day training. Having a protocol written prior to the start of training (and intervention) is helpful to ensure that everyone is clear about what will be done and that there are no questions from those implementing the training. If all adults are on the same page and well prepared, the chances of success are greater.

Student Training Protocol

Two 15-minute training sessions. Day One:

- Alex and Anastasia introduce the tootling procedure as something students will do in class.
- Provide verbal examples of prosocial behaviors.
- Ask students to give their own examples of how they help others at home and at school.
- Ask students to provide examples of how they help or be kind to each other.
- Define tattling (telling the teacher when a peer did something wrong) and tootling (telling the teacher when a peer did something helpful or being kind to others).
- Give students examples of tootling (e.g., helping a student pick up their books, loaning a student a pencil, showing a student how to work a math problem).
- Have students provide their own examples.
- Praise examples that fit criteria for tootling; give corrective feedback when students give examples that do not fit the criteria
- Remind students that we will review this tomorrow before we begin.

Day Two

- Define tootling as reporting when peers do something helpful or are kind to others.
- Remind students that tootling does not involve reporting their own behaviors, just their classmates' prosocial behaviors.
- Remind students that they are only to report peers for helping classmates, not their teacher or other adults.

- Pass out index cards and have students write down examples of tootling: Who (classmate) did what (helpful behavior), and for whom (who they helped). Students may choose to use "Box check" cards instead of writing.
- Collect examples.
- Read examples aloud and provide praise for examples that fit criteria; corrective feedback for examples that do not fit criteria.

Collecting baseline: It is important to collect information related to student behaviors prior to the start of the intervention in order to determine if tootling has an impact on student performance. This is relatively simple and can be accomplished in numerous ways, depending on your goals.

Setting the goal: Once you have an understanding of how often your target behaviors occur, you can determine an appropriate goal for students to work toward. The goal you set should be ambitious, but also obtainable.

Starting Intervention

Tootling

After all staff and students are trained and baseline data have been collected, it is time to get started! The remainder of this chapter will outline the steps for implementation.

1 **Prepare all materials**. Be sure to have all materials ready before students begin tootling. Create the tootle cards, and make sure they are somewhere that children can access them. Place the tootle box (where children will put completed tootles) somewhere in the room where everyone can see it. Be sure to prepare how you will track tootles and have that prominently displayed in the classroom.
2 **Set the goal**. It is important to set the goal prior to starting the intervention so that all of the children know how many tootles are needed to earn a reward. As discussed earlier, the goal should be ambitious, but achievable. Use the baseline data that was collected to determine what an appropriate goal will be. Share the goal with the students and explain how they can keep track of their progress.
3 **Choose the reward**. As discussed earlier, it is important for the children to be motivated to participate in tootling. The best way to get kids engaged, at least initially, is to provide a motivating reward.
4 **Start Tootling.** On the first day of tootling, remind students about the training and how to tootle. Be sure to set the parameters of the intervention. For example, will the students tootle all day, or just during certain times? Can students tootle about any behavior they see or only behaviors that were discussed during training.
5 **Encourage students to tootle throughout the day**. Remind students throughout the day to tootle. It will be especially important at the

beginning of implementation to make sure that students engage in the intervention.

6 **Tootle review meeting**. Choose a time of day to review the tootles. Typically, this occurs either at the end of the day or the beginning of the next day. During this time the tootles that were written should be read to the group. Individual students who wrote tootles, as well as those that received tootles should be given praise. After the individual tootles are highlighted, they should be counted and added to the tootle count. As discussed earlier, the total should be publicly posted. This should be repeated every day until the group meets the tootle goal.

7 **Provide the reward**. Once the group reaches the predetermined number of tootles, the chosen reward should be given as soon as possible. If the reward is something that can be provided right away (e.g., candy, toy), that is ideal. If it is not something that can be given right away, like an end of day activity, the group should be told when they will get the reward. It is extremely important that if the reward is delayed, it is given at the time promised. This can be hard at times, given the unpredictable nature of schedule in schools, but if students earn the reward and then don't get it there will be little motivation to continue tootling.

8 **Revise the goal.** After the group meets the goal, it should be reset. Depending on the group and how long it took to meet the previous goal, it is good to consider if the goal should be raised. Each new goal would ideally be slightly higher than the last, continuing to challenge the group. If, however, the group had a difficult time meeting the goal, increasing the goal may not be appropriate at that time. If the group isn't writing enough tootles to meet the goal at a reasonable amount of time, it is possible that changes will need to be made to the intervention. Chapter 10 discusses how to troubleshoot if the intervention is not working as planned.

This chapter has described the basics of how to implement the tootling intervention. This, along with previous chapters, should provide you with all the information needed to successfully begin tootling. The remaining chapters provide an overview of how to adapt tootling for different ages, and settings. It also provides information related to how best to implement and how to make adjustments if needed.

References

Cashwell, T. H., Skinner, C. H., & Smith, E. S. (2001). Increasing second-grade students' reports of peers' prosocial behaviors via direct instruction, group reinforcement, and progress feedback: A replication and extension. *Education & Treatment of Children*, 24(2), 161–175. https://www.jstor.org/stable/42899652.

Cihak, D. F., Kirk, E. R., & Boon, R. T. (2009). Effects of classwide positive peer "tootling" to reduce the disruptive classroom behaviors of elementary students with and without disabilities. *Journal of Behavioral Education*, 18(4), 267–278. https://doi. org/10.1007/s10864-009-9091-8.

Lambert, A. M., Tingstrom, D. H., Sterling, H. E., Dufrene, B. A., & Lynne, S. (2015). Effects of tootling on classwide disruptive and appropriate behavior of upper-elementary students. *Behavior Modification*, 39(3), 413–430. https://doi.org/ 10.1177/0145445514566506.

Lum, J. D. K., Tingstrom, D. H., Dufrene, B. A., Radley, K. C., & Lynne, S. (2017). Effects of tootling on classwide disruptive and academically engaged behavior of general-education high school students. *Psychology in the Schools*, 54(4), 370–384. https:// doi.org/10.1002/pits.22002.

7 Data Collection

Alexandra Hilt-Panahon and Kennedi Alstead

Data Collection

As discussed in previous chapters, collecting accurate and reliable data related to the behaviors you are hoping to change will have a significant impact on the effectiveness of any intervention that is put in place. This chapter will describe a variety of ways to gather objective information related to both the reasons for problem behaviors in the classroom as well as the effectiveness of the tootling and other interventions. The chapter is constructed to first review methods for gathering data that will help to provide insight into the reasons that problems may be occurring in the classroom. Next, we will look at how to accurately record the occurrences of both problem and appropriate behaviors to establish baseline. Finally, we will review the importance of maintaining data collection practices from baseline to intervention.

Before implementing tootling, it is helpful to gather as much information about the students' behavior and the environment in which behaviors occur. By having a detailed picture of what is happening in the classroom, you can more easily design the tootling intervention to best meet the needs of those involved. It is important to remember that different types of data will provide different types of information that can reveal important information to assist with all aspects of intervention implementation. Before trying to start an intervention, the main goal of the data is to understand the WHY of the behavior. Why is this happening? Why are students behaving the way to they do? The data collection methods described in the following section will describe a variety of ways to gather data that will help to answer the WHY.

Operational Definition of Behavior

To conduct observations you first need to develop an operational definition of the target behavior. An operational definition is defined as a description of "something in terms of the operations (procedures, actions, or processes) by which it could be observed and measured" by the APA dictionary of Psychology (American Psychological Association, n.d.) When referring to a specific behavior, the operational definition provides a description of what the behavior looks like for a

DOI: 10.4324/9781003128663-9

particular person or persons. For example, if a student is referred to by his teacher as "aggressive," what does that mean? Aggression can take many forms, and one person's idea of aggressive behavior may look very different than someone else's. In order to avoid any confusion or inconsistency in how we evaluate the behavior, an operational definition is necessary. So, rather than simply saying a student is aggressive, it is much more useful to define what that behavior looks like for that particular student. Some examples of possible operational definitions of "aggression" are provided below:

- The student demonstrates aggressive behavior, which includes slapping, kicking, and biting adults and peers.
- Aggressive behavior includes throwing objects at peers when approached.
- Aggression is defined as shouting obscenities at teachers, spitting, and destroying property.

From these three examples, it is clear the aggression can mean lots of different things. If someone was asked to conduct an observation of a student and told to look for aggression, what would they look for? By having a specific operational definition, the guess work is removed. Anyone observing the student knowing that they are looking for "slapping, kicking, and biting adults and peers" will be able to accurately record those behaviors.

Anecdotal Reports

While it is often very easy to identify that an intervention is needed, it is harder to pinpoint the exact reasons for the problem behavior and why intervention is needed. In order to identify the precise problems and the best remedies, it is often helpful to gather information from a variety of sources to determine what the main problems are and what to target in intervention. It is recommended that key stakeholders provide input related to any and all concerns. This may include conversations or formal interviews with other teachers, previous teachers, parents, counselors, and the student themselves. Each person can provide a unique perspective on the concerns for the child and can assist with choosing the appropriate intervention and how it should be designed.

Anecdotal information from individuals that know the child the best will help to provide the context for the behaviors in need of intervention. In addition, situations in which the child is able to demonstrate success may be identified. This will assist in intervention planning. This process will allow the intervention team to refine the operational definition to be as precise as possible.

Narrative observations

A slightly more structured method of data collection is to conduct a narrative observation. This allows you to evaluate the "big picture" related to the students, problem behaviors, and the environment in which they occur.

Narrative observations seek to provide a record of all that occurs in the setting in which problem behaviors occur. When conducting a narrative observation, it is important to record all the details of the situation including the who, what, where, why, and how.

Before starting your observation, write down the date, time, setting, and people that are present. This should include the adults and children that are part of the environment at that time. It is also important to record the activity the students are engaged in at the beginning of the observation. As you begin the observation, record as much detail as possible related to what is happening and the interactions that occur. If anything changes, such as the activity or personnel, that should be recorded as well. Finally, it is important to record positive behaviors and interactions in addition to problematic situations as this can be valuable to creating a positive environment. It is helpful to conduct multiple narrative observations over a variety of situations and settings. This will provide a complete picture of the students, the environment, and any potential triggers for problem behavior.

The following excerpt is an example of several narrative observations of a student named Tasha in her reading and math classes.

3/10/2021

Reading: Ms.Florendo

9:05 All students entered class and sat at their seats. There are 22 students in the classroom with one teacher. Each student had a bin on their desk with materials to begin working. Students appeared to know what was expected and immediately took out their materials and began working independently. The teacher circulated throughout the classroom and provided assistance to students as needed. Tasha requested help 3 times during the work period. The teacher responded quickly and Tasha returned to work. The students worked in this fashion until the teacher asked them to clean up.

9:15 All students turned attention to the teacher at the front of the room. The teacher began the lesson with a review of the last lesson. The students had numerous opportunities to participate. Tasha volunteered to answer 8/10 questions asked. She was called on once and answered correctly. The teacher praised her for the correct response. The teacher then introduced new material. She modeled the skill and then provided examples for the class. Tasha was attentive throughout this period.

9:25 The teacher then provided opportunity for the students to work in small groups to practice the skill. Tasha sat with two other students during this activity. The other two students immediately began to work on the assignment given, while Tasha sat with her hands folded and did not appear to attend. The teacher was circulating around the room and noticed that Tasha was not working. She came over to the group and provided a reminder to the group (to Tasha) of what the assignment was. She reminded them that this was practice and that they may not get all the answers right, but that they needed to try. She then worked the first problem with the group. After this Tasha participated with her classmates until the end of the class period.

3/10/2021

Math: Ms. Winkler

9:50 The students entered the room and stated talking with each other about various non-school related topics. The teacher said good morning and that she would be right with them. She told them to "get ready". The students continued to talk and move slowly toward their desks. There were 22 students in the class. Tasha was very talkative. She was talking with three other girls.

9:52 The students were still talking. The teacher told them to take out their books. The students continued to talk. 17/22 students got their books out. The teacher was looking through papers on her desks. She continued to look at her work while the students talked and waited.

9:56 The teacher got up from her desk and said "Are we ready to get started?" She began with a lesson of new material. She lectured to the students about the concept. Students sat and listened, but did not have a lot of opportunities to participate or ask questions. Tasha appeared attentive throughout the lecture. She was oriented toward the teacher and writing notes in her notebook.

10:20 The teacher finished her lecture and then asked if there were any questions. No one had any. The teacher then gave out a worksheet and told the students to complete the problems until the end of class. After the papers were passed out the teacher sat back down at her desk and started paperwork while the students worked independently at their desks. Tasha looked at the worksheet for about a minute and then put it down and began looking around the room. After a few minutes she looked at the paper again, but quickly put it down and sat quietly until the end of the period.

Now that you have read the scenarios, consider the following questions:

1   What does the reading classroom look like?

   a   What positive things are in place?
   b   What could be improved?

2   What does the math class look like?

   a   What positive things are in place?
   b   What could be improved?

3   How do the students behave in each of the classes?
4   What are your overall takeaways from the observations?

As can be seen through this example, there is a lot to be learned from these types of observations. Observations like these should ideally be done by someone not typically part of the classroom environment. While having a visitor in the classroom can cause some disruption, it is the best way to see what typically happens day to day. We will discuss ways to address the effects of observers in the classroom later in this chapter. As a visitor to the classroom, you can gather a lot of information about the students, staff, and how things are run. This information can be valuable to the intervention team when determining what needs to be put in place before, during, and in addition to the tootling intervention.

Generally, it appears that Ms. Florendo's reading class is well structured. She has clear expectations for the students and they know what to do. She is able to maintain order and keep students engaged throughout the work period. In contrast, Ms. Winkler's classroom does not appear to have the same level of structure. The students enter the room in a somewhat chaotic manner and that continues as the class period goes on. She does not set specific expectations for how the students should behave, and if she did, they are not enforced. As a result, the students do not engage, interact, or attend in this class at the same level as they did in reading. Given that this is the same group of students, it allows us to see how the environment effects behavior.

When we look specifically at Tasha, the target of these observations, we can see differences in her behavior as well. In Ms. Florendo's classroom Tasha is generally on-task and attentive to the teacher. When she does get off-task, Ms. Florendo is able to redirect her with a quick review of the expectations for the assignment. In Ms. Winkler's class, Tasha gets off-task easily and remains so throughout the independent work period because there are no consequences for this behavior. So, from this information we can identify the problem behavior (off-task), develop a definition (looking around the room, oriented away from work), and begin to hypothesize possible reasons for the behavior observed (directions are not clear to Tasha, lack of interest in completing the assignment).

It is important to note that these conclusions are drawn from one observation in each setting. Best practice dictates that multiple observations be conducted in order to ensure an accurate representation of the environment and the students in it. If similar behaviors were seen over a series of narrative observations, conclusions could be made about how best to improve the performance of the students, specifically Tasha, in each of the settings.

ABC data collection

A similar, but more structured way to collect data is to conduct an Antecedent-Behavior-Consequence (ABC) observation. The narrative observations help to provide a big picture overview of the situation, while ABC observations help to pinpoint why the problem behavior occurs. These observations are structured around a specific behaviors and the triggers and outcomes of those behaviors.

Once an operational definition has been established, the observations can begin. To conduct an ABC observation, begin by making four columns on a piece of paper. Label the first column as TIME, the second as ANTECEDENT the third column as BEHAVIOR, and the last column as CONSEQUENCE. Note all information about the observation including the date, time, activity, and teacher at the top of the paper. During the observation, you should record all behaviors of interest along with what happened right before the behavior (the antecedent) and what happens as a result of the behavior (the consequence). An example is provided below.

Table 7.1 Antecedent-Behavior-Consequence Data Collection Sheet

Date:	Activity:	Teacher:	Target student:
Time	**Antecedent**	**Behavior**	**Consequence**

Notes:

The following is an example of an ABC observation with the student we looked at earlier, Tasha.

Table 7.2 Antecedent-Behavior-Consequence Data Collection Sheet

Date: 9/11/22	Activity: Math	Teacher: Ms. Winkler	Target student: Tasha
Time	**Antecedent**	**Behavior**	**Consequence**
9:50		Students walk in to room	Teacher working at her desk
	Teacher asks students to sit down and take out books	Students continue talking	Teacher continues work at her desk
9:55	Teacher walks to front of room and asks students to sit down and take out books	15/22 sit and take out books Tasha sits down at desk but does not take out book	Teacher begins lesson

	Teacher lectures students	*Tasha looks around the room, taps her pencil, no book on her desk*	*Teacher continues lesson*
10:10	*Teacher asks students if they have any questions*	*2 students ask a question Tasha doesn't ask any questions*	*Teacher answers questions*
	Teacher tells students to complete worksheet provided	*Students start working Tasha looks at paper then puts it down, looks around the room*	*Teacher sits down at her desk and opens her computer*

Looking at this observation in conjunction with the narrative observations conducted previously, patterns in Tasha's behavior begin to be emerge. It appears that when given work in math, Tasha does not participate. This also happened in reading, but when her teacher intervened, Tasha completed the work. In math class, however, Ms. Winkler does not acknowledge when Tasha is off-task. This allows Tasha to remain off-task for long periods of time.

ABC observations provide interventionists with specific, detailed information about the events that lead to target behaviors as well as how individuals react to those behaviors in different environments. Understanding the antecedents and consequences to a behavior can aid in the development of effective interventions.

Scatterplot data

A scatterplot analysis is another useful data collection tool that can provide a range of information related to the problem behaviors of a student. Scatterplots give unique insight into when behaviors are most likely to occur. To conduct a scatterplot analysis, begin by creating a datasheet. Datasheets can be formatted in a variety of ways, but typically capture data across multiple days or weeks. Data are collected based on a specific timeframe and/or activity schedule. An example of a scatterplot data sheet is provided below.

Table 7.3 Scatterplot Data

Dates:	Data Collected by:		Target Student:		
Time/Activity	Monday	Tuesday	Wednesday	Thursday	Friday

Dates:		Data Collected by:		Target Student:	
Time/Activity	Monday	Tuesday	Wednesday	Thursday	Friday

To collect the data, the target student should be observed throughout the day. Each day is broken down into intervals and data are recorded when and if target behaviors are observed during a particular interval. So, if someone sees the behavior occur during a particular interval, the box for that interval is checked. By recording the intervals in which the behavior occurs across time, patterns will often emerge that identifies when problem behavior is most likely to occur.

An example of a scatterplot for Tasha is provided below. Ms. Devlin, the school social worker and a member of the intervention team at Tasha's school, decided that it would be helpful to collect these data across the week to pinpoint the most problematic activities and times of day. During a conversation with Tasha's teacher, she also learned that Tasha has a difficult time interacting with her peers. She tends to stay to herself when in social situations. When peers try to engage her in activities, she will either ignore them, yell at them to "go away," or leave her alone. Ms. Devlin thought it would be important to look at this behavior too since it could seriously impact Tasha's ability to make and keep friends. The results of the observations are provided here.

Table 7.4 Scatterplot Data

Dates: 3/14-18/2022		Data Collected by: Ms. Devlin			Target Student: Tasha	
Target Behavior: Off-task behavior (X)– Tasha is oriented away from the teacher or work, looking around the room, tapping pencil Anti-social behavior (O) – staying to herself during social activities, yelling at peers to go away						
Time/Activity	Monday	Tuesday	Wednesday	Thursday	Friday
8:30 Morning meeting	X			X	
9:00 Reading			X		
9:30 Reading					
10:00 Math	X	X			X
10:30 Math	X	X	X	X	X
11:00 Math	X	X	X	X	X
11:30 Lunch	O	O	O	O	O
12:00 Recess	O	O	O	O	O
12:30 Writing	X				
1:00 Science	X				
1:30 Specials					
2:00 Specials					
2:30 Afternoon meeting	X			X	
3:00 Dismissal					

After reviewing Tasha's scatterplot, it becomes clear that several patterns emerge. First, consistent with the narrative observations that were conducted, Tasha consistently goes off-task during math class. The behavior does occasionally happen in other class too, however; the behavior consistently occurs in math. Another interesting pattern is that Tasha demonstrates "anti-social" behavior every day during lunch and recess. Given the social nature of both activities, it makes sense that these behaviors would not have been seen during academic classes but are seen during lunch and recess.

So, to summarize what has been learned about Tasha's behavior so far, it appears that Tasha is most often and consistently off-task during math class. In addition, she tends to keep to herself during social situations such as lunch and recess. While this information is helpful, there are also lots of questions that still need to be answered. For example, we do not know anything related to how much the behaviors in question occur. Multiple questions related to Tasha's behaviors can be developed based on what has already be learned. Some of the questions are listed below:

1 How many times each class period does Tasha go off-task?
2 How long does she stay off-task?

3   Are there specific activities during math class that she goes off-task?
4   Is she "anti-social" with all peers or only some peers?
5   Are there activities or individuals with whom she will interact?

All of these questions can be answered using various methods of data collection that will be addressed in the next section.

Event Based Recording

Frequency. Frequency recording is a relatively simple and easy way to gather important information related to the student and their problem behavior. To gather these data, an observer only needs to count the number of times the target behavior occurs. This can be done in a variety of ways, from a simple tally on a piece of paper to gathering data using a computer program designed for this purpose. Collecting frequency data provides an objective measure of the behavior. It allows us to see how much and how often a problem behavior occurs. In addition, it helps to evaluate the effectiveness of intervention by comparing frequency of behavior before and after intervention is implemented.

Rate. Rate is the frequency with which a target behavior occurs within the context of time. Rather than simply reporting how many times a behavior occurs, rate provides a timeframe in addition to the number of instances of behavior. Data are reported in terms of the number of behaviors that occur within a specific amount of time. So, we can understand how often behaviors occur within a minute, an hour, or any predetermined time period. Rate based data reporting helps us to make comparisons across multiple observations by standardizing the frequency of occurrences, regardless of the time observed.

Time Based Recording

Latency. Latency measures the amount of time from a request or command to the start of a behavior (Richards, Taylor, & Ramasamy, 2014). This measure can be helpful when you want to know how long it takes a student to begin to engage in a task or activity. These data are collected by recording the time when a demand is made and stop timing when the student starts the task. This will provide not only the amount of time it takes a student to engage in the activity, but also the percentage of compliance. This can be helpful as you evaluate the effectiveness of an intervention aimed at increasing compliance and decreasing time to compliance.

Duration. Duration recording captures the length of time a behavior occurs. Data are collected by timing how long a student engages in the target behavior. So, the observer would begin timing at the start of the behavior and continue until the behavior ends. By recording time engaged in the behavior, the observer can get an overall understanding of how much time is spent engaged in the target behavior, as well as the average length of engagement for each occurrence.

The following is an example of a situation in which duration recording would be useful for the purpose of understanding the problem behavior.

> George is a ten-year-old student in general education. George has been having difficulty staying on task during math. The intervention specialist at the school, Ms. Bennet, was asked to observe George to determine how much time he is on-task. Ms. Bennet decides to use whole interval recording to make this determination. She knows that math class runs for 45 minutes, so she decides to observe for the entire class period. Before starting observations, Ms. Bennett was careful to operationally define on-task behavior using information gathered from his teachers and anecdotal observations of George. Using the operational definition as her guide, Ms. Bennett watched George during his math class over multiple days. At the beginning of math class, she started a time. Anytime she saw that he was on-task, she noted the time. When he engaged in behavior that did not meet the definition of on-task she again noted the time. At the end of the class period, Ms. Bennett had a record of George's on-task behavior.

Below are the data that were collected during the first observation conducted by Ms. Bennett.

Table 7.5 Duration Datasheet

Dates: 6/22/2021		Data Collected by: *Ms. Bennett*		Target Student: *George*
Target Behavior: *On-task– George is oriented toward the teacher or work, or engaged in the assigned activity.*				
Event	Start Time	End Time	Duration	Notes
1	:36	1:29	53 sec	*George stopped writing; Looking around the room*
2	3:16	7:44	4 min 28 sec	*Teacher lecturing*
3	8:04	12:22	4 min 18 sec	*Teacher redirected George at 8:04*
4	12:35	18:55	6 min 20 sec	*Teacher asked students to complete independent work at 17:45*
5	24:35	26:47	2 min 12 sec	*Redirect at 24:35*
6	33:16	36:58	3 min 42 sec	*Redirect 33:15*
7	41:25	45:00	3 min 35 sec	*Teacher ended lesson and explained homework Class ended at 45:00*
			Duration Total : *25min 28 sec* *57% of class on-task*	

As we can see from the data provided above, there is a great deal we can learn George's on- (and off-) task behavior. Not only can we determine how much of class time was spent on- and off- task, we also have a picture of how often he goes off-task and the activities that may keep him engaged.

Interval Recording

Interval recording provides an approximation of the number of times that a behavior occurs (Alberto & Troutman, 2013). While it is not as accurate as collecting exact occurrences, it provide a reasonable approximation of behavior and is a manageable method of data collection, especially for teachers and other professionals. To implement interval recording, a predetermined amount of time is designated for the observation. That amount of time is then divided into equal intervals and behavior is recorded if and when the behavior occurs. The following section will describe the interval recording options available.

Table 7.6 Interval Data Sheet

1	2	3	4	5	6	7	8	9	10
11	12	13	14	15	16	17	18	19	20
21	22	23	24	25	26	27	28	29	30
31	32	33	34	35	36	37	38	39	40
41	42	43	44	45	46	47	48	49	50
51	52	53	54	55	56	57	58	59	60
61	62	63	64	65	66	67	68	69	70
71	72	73	74	75	76	77	78	79	80
81	82	83	84	85	86	87	88	89	90
91	92	93	94	95	96	97	98	99	100

Whole interval. In whole interval recording, the behavior is recorded as present if it occurs throughout the entire interval. For this reason, choosing an appropriate length for the interval is important. If intervals are too long, it will be very difficult to accurately record the level of the target behavior. If the interval is set for 10 minutes and the student engages in the behavior for 9 minutes and 55 seconds, but stops 5 seconds before end of the interval, the behavior would not be recorded as present. The shorter the interval, the more accurate the estimate of the behavior.

Short intervals may be problematic too also, however. Recording data in short intervals can be difficult, especially for novel data collectors. It is important to determine the shortest interval that is feasible while still allowing for accurate recording. The following is an example of whole interval recording.

> George is a ten-year-old student in general education. George has been having difficulty staying on task during math. The intervention specialist at the school, Ms. Bennet, was asked to observe George to determine how much time he is on-task. Ms. Bennet decides to use whole interval recording to make this determination. She knows that math class runs for 45 minutes, so she decides to observe for the entire class period. She wants to make sure she has an accurate representation of his on-task behavior, so she decides to divide the observation period into short intervals and record if he remains on task throughout each interval. She decides that 10 seconds is an appropriate amount of time for each interval to allow her to get a good estimate of his on-task behavior. Throughout the class period, Ms. Bennett watches George and records if he was on-task during the entire interval. She has set a repeating 10 second timer on her phone that vibrates. Each time she feels the vibration, she records a (+) if George was on-task throughout the previous interval and a (−) if he was not. The following data sheets shows the result of her observations.

Table 7.7 Whole Interval Recording

1–1	1–2	2–1	2–2	3–1	3–2	4–1	4–2	5–1	5–2
							X	X	X
6–1	6–2	7–1	7–2	8–1	8–2	9–1	9–2	10–1	10–2
X	X	X	X	X			X	X	X
11–1	11–2	12–1	12–2	13–1	13–2	14–1	14–2	15–1	15–2
X	X	X	X			X	X	X	X
16–1	16–2	17–1	17–2	18–1	18–2	19–1	19–2	20–1	20–2
X	X	X	X	X					
21–1	21–2	22–1	22–2	23–1	23–2	24–1	24–2	25–1	25–2
26–1	26–2	27–1	27–2	28–1	28–2	29–1	29–2	30–1	30–2
X	X	X							
31–1	31–2	32–1	32–2	33–1	33–2	34–1	34–2	35–1	35–2
							X	X	X
36–1	36–2	37–1	37–2	38–1	38–2	39–1	39–2	40–1	40–2
X									
41–1	41–2	42–1	42–2	43–1	43–2	44–1	44–2		
	X	X	X	X	X	X	X		

Partial interval. Partial interval recording is very similar to whole interval in that the observation period is divided into intervals, and behavior is recorded as present if it occurs within the interval. The difference in partial interval, is that the behavior is recorded as present if it occurs at any point during the interval. So, the behavior does not need to occur for the entire time period, it only needs to occur at some point during the interval. To see the contrast, here are George's data if Ms. Bennett had collected partial interval instead of whole interval.

Table 7.8 Partial Interval Recording

1–1	1–2	2–1	2–2	3–1	3–2	4–1	4–2	5–1	5–2
	X	X				X	X	X	X
6–1	6–2	7–1	7–2	8–1	8–2	9–1	9–2	10–1	10–2
X	X	X	X	X	X	X	X	X	X
11–1	11–2	12–1	12–2	13–1	13–2	14–1	14–2	15–1	15–2
X	X	X	X	X	X	X	X	X	X
16–1	16–2	17–1	17–2	18–1	18–2	19–1	19–2	20–1	20–2
X	X	X	X	X	X	X	X		
21–1	21–2	22–1	22–2	23–1	23–2	24–1	24–2	25–1	25–2
								X	X
26–1	26–2	27–1	27–2	28–1	28–2	29–1	29–2	30–1	30–2
X	X	X	X						
31–1	31–2	32–1	32–2	33–1	33–2	34–1	34–2	35–1	35–2
						X	X	X	X
36–1	36–2	37–1	37–2	38–1	38–2	39–1	39–2	40–1	40–2
X	X	X	X						
41–1	41–2	42–1	42–2	43–1	43–2	44–1	44–2		
	X	X	X	X	X	X	X		

Momentary Time Sampling. Momentary Time Sampling (MTS) is the final form of interval recording that will be discussed. In Momentary Time Sampling, the observer once again determines the length of the observation and divides the time into equal intervals. Unlike whole and partial interval recording, the student is not observed throughout the interval. Instead, at the end of each interval the observer looks at the student and determines if they are engaged in the target behavior at that time. If the student is engaging in the target behavior at that specific point in time, the behavior is recorded as present. If they are not engaged in the behavior when the interval ends, it is not recorded. An example of George's behavior recorded using Momentary Time Sampling is provided below.

Table 7.9 Momentary Time Sampling

1–1	1–2	2–1	2–2	3–1	3–2	4–1	4–2	5–1	5–2
	X					X	X	X	X
6–1	6–2	7–1	7–2	8–1	8–2	9–1	9–2	10–1	10–2
X	X	X	X	X		X	X	X	X
11–1	11–2	12–1	12–2	13–1	13–2	14–1	14–2	15–1	15–2
X	X	X	X	X	X	X	X	X	X
16–1	16–2	17–1	17–2	18–1	18–2	19–1	19–2	20–1	20–2
X	X	X	X	X	X	X	X		
21–1	21–2	22–1	22–2	23–1	23–2	24–1	24–2	25–1	25–2
26–1	26–2	27–1	27–2	28–1	28–2	29–1	29–2	30–1	30–2
X	X	X	X						
31–1	31–2	32–1	32–2	33–1	33–2	34–1	34–2	35–1	35–2
							X	X	X
36–1	36–2	37–1	37–2	38–1	38–2	39–1	39–2	40–1	40–2
X	X	X	X						
41–1	41–2	42–1	42–2	43–1	43–2	44–1	44–2		
			X	X	X	X	X		

All three of these examples use the same observation, just using different recording methods. As we can see, when the actual duration of on-task behavior is observed, George is on-task for 57% of the class period. With interval recordings, we are observing the number of intervals a behavior occurs, not the actual amount of time spent engaged in that behavior. Therefore, we are evaluating an estimate of the amount of behavior as opposed to an actual behavioral count. Given that interval recordings are estimates of total behavior, we can evaluate the accuracy of these estimates using this example.

Looking at the hole interval recording we can see that George was on-task for the entire interval for 38/88 intervals, or 43% of observed intervals. This is a much lower estimate of total behavior than actually occurred. Unfortunately, whole interval does tend to underestimate behavior as much of the data is "lost" when it does not occur for the entire interval. As a result, whole interval recording is recommended only for behaviors that last for an extended period of time. In addition, it is recommended that the length of the interval be as short as possible in order to capture the greatest amount of behavior. For example, if we look at the first 2 minutes of the observation we see that George was on-task for a total of 53 seconds. Using whole interval recording, however, there are no intervals in which George was on-task for the entire interval. Therefore, no behavior is recorded. If the observer had

Table 7.10 Comparison of Data Collection Methods

Duration Recording:

1	:36	1:29	53 sec	*George stopped writing; Looking around the room*

Whole Interval (30 Second Intervals):

1–1	1–2	2–1	2–2
-	-	-	-

Whole Interval (10 Second Intervals):

1–1	1–2	1–3	1–4	1–5	1–6	2–1	2–2	2–3	2–4	2–5	2–6
-	-	-	-	+	+	+	+	-	-	-	-

used shorter intervals, perhaps 10 seconds instead of 30 seconds, we would have a more accurate estimate of George's behavior.

Partial interval recording tends to be more accurate than whole interval recording, although it can overestimate behavior at time. Because the behavior only has to occur for at some point during the interval, it counts the same whether it occurs for 1 second or 30 seconds. This can be combatted by putting duration parameters in the operational definition. Such as "the student is on-task if she is oriented toward the teacher and/or the assigned task for at least 5 seconds." Partial interval is one of the most widely used measures in classrooms due to the ease of data collection and relative accuracy. It is particularly useful when gathering data related to discrete behaviors.

Things to Consider

Who will collect the data? The first thing to consider when deciding to gather data is to determine who will collect those data. It is important to ensure that whoever will be collecting data is well trained, fully understands the operational definition, and has the time to devote to data collection. When possible, it is best to have someone that is not typically in the environment collect data. While it may be problematic initially to have a novel person in the room, this typically doesn't last too long and allows for someone who does not interact with students typically to record all data. Assigning one or more people to gather data is important, but it must also be considered how these temporary duties may impact that individuals other responsibilities.

How often will data be collected? Once the data collector or collectors are identified, the next step is to determine a schedule for data collection. It is important to gather enough information to make the data useful, but in an efficient manner that does not waste the time for the staff or students. This is where the preliminary data that were collected earlier will be useful. By reviewing data collected through anecdotal means as well as scatterplot, it can be determined when the best time of day to observe will be. It should also be decided ahead of time how long data collection sessions will be and how many times a day. It will be important to remain as consistent as possible related to time and settings in which observations are conducted. This allows for comparisons across days. It also provides the opportunity to evaluate how a student behaves in different environments.

How long will data be collected? Another question that should be answered before the start of data collection is for how long data be collected. This can be a tricky question to answer, because you want to ensure you have enough data to make an informed decision, but also not take too much time until intervention is implemented. We also want to know quickly if intervention isn't working so adjustments can be made. For this reason, frequent data collection is better to allow for the maximum amount of data to be collected in the shortest amount of time.

Variables that may affect data collection. Finally, it is important to be aware of the effects of having an observer enter the environment. Whenever someone new is introduced to an environment, it changes that environment and can have temporary and/or permanent effects on how individuals behave. It is important to take this into consideration when evaluating student behavior during observations. The following variables may influence observations and should be considered and minimized to the greatest extent possible.

- **Reactivity.** Reactivity refers to how the target student, as well as other individuals in the observational setting respond to being observed (Repp, et al., 1988). Despite our best efforts, students often know when they are being watched, and may change their behavior as a result. In addition, often others in an environment may change their behavior when others are present, and this change may impact the target student's behavior either positively or negatively. For example, teachers may change the amount of free time provided to students during a class period if the principal is in the classroom observing. Likewise, a student may be less likely to engage in a problem behavior when a novel person is present. In order to address the problem of reactivity there are several things that can be done to lessen its effects. First, having the individual that is chosen to observe be familiar to the students in the classroom can help to reduce reactivity. While it may not be a person who is regularly in the classroom, if the person is someone students know they will be less likely to behave differently in their presence. Another way to combat reactivity effects is to have the observer spend time in the target environment prior to the start of formal observations. If the observer can spend some time in the classroom prior to observations, they become a member of that environment. Students will feel more comfortable when the visit and be more likely to behave in a manner that is typical.

- **Expectancy.** This refers to the expectations of the observer for the student and how those expectations may affect the way a person views a situation. This may lead to bias in how behavior is interpreted. This bias may cause target behaviors to be over or underestimated. For example, if a teacher knows that a child will be remove from their classroom if they don't respond well to an intervention they may be less likely to see positive change in student behavior. Likewise, if the teacher is highly invested in a student, they may evaluate behavior more favorably to ensure the best outcome for the student. None of this is necessarily intentional, it is simply a product of natural biases that may impact our perceptions of a situation. The best way to combat expectancy is to enlist an observer that does not have preconceived biases or favored outcomes. This can, at times, be hard to do but is preferred if possible. Another way to combat expectancy is to have very clear operational definitions of target behaviors (see above) and have more than one observer if possible. This will decrease the likelihood that an individual's biases will impact outcomes.

- **Complexity.** A third variable that may affect the accuracy of direct observations is the complexity of the data collection system. If the behaviors in question are ill defined, difficult to observe, or there are too many to observe at one time it may impact how accurate the data collector may be in their observations. To avoid this threat to accurate data collection, it is best to limit the number of students and behaviors that are being observed at any given time. In addition, clearly define any and all behaviors that will be recorded during observations.

- **Observer Drift.** The final variable that may impact the validity of direct observations is observer drift. Observer drift refers to the tendency of observers to change how they apply the definitions of behavior over time (Kazdin, 1977). Initially, observers are trained on the operational definition of the target behavior and typically practice observing that behavior to ensure accuracy. Over time, however, individual observers may drift away from the original definition and begin to record the presence or absence of the behavior differently than described in the definition.

Example. Teachers in a middle school decide to observe a student to determine how often he gets out of his seat in different classes. The students' teachers all discuss what getting out of seat looks like and determine an operation definition. They define out of seat is defined as "removing his buttocks from the seat of the chair and standing at his desk or walking around the room". All of the teachers agree to this definition. Ms. Bellows begins to observe the student using the agreed upon definition. After several days, however, she notices that he doesn't always stand up all the way. Sometimes he lifts his buttocks off the seat and puts his feet on the chair. Even though it doesn't follow the definition exactly, Ms. Bellows decides that this is also getting out of seat and begins counting this as out of seat behavior as well.

At the end of the week, the teachers all get together to discuss the results of their observations. When they all compare their findings, Ms. Bellows has a much higher number of out of seat behaviors than the other teachers. During their discussion of when he would get out of his seat, Ms. Bellows mentioned that she really didn't like it when he puts his feet on the chair with his bottom in the air. She stated that he did that the most. The other teachers looked confused and asked her what she meant. She explained that the behavior bothered her so she started counting that too.

As we can see from this example, that fact that Ms. Bellows changed the operational definition affected the outcome of her observations. This drift away from the original operational definition was not done intentionally. Ms.

Bellows likely felt she was gathering more accurate data by including the additional behaviors in the definition. As we can see, though, her data were different from the other teachers and does not accurately reflect the number of times he was out of seat according to the original definition.

It is important to remember that different data collection methods serve different purposes and choosing the best option for each situation is important to overall success. The most important thing to consider when choosing a data collection method is the purpose of the data. Why are data being collected and how will it be used? As outlined above, anecdotal and narrative data collection is used to gather general information about the behavior and the environment in which it occurs. Data that capture the antecedent and consequences to behavior, such as ABC and Scatterplots, help to identify why behaves occur and what maintains them. Finally, event and time based data provide a record of how much behaviors occur both before intervention is put in place as well as after.

This chapter has summarized multiple methods of collecting data within an educational setting. When evaluating the research on Tootling, partial interval and momentary time sampling data are most often used (Lum et al., 2017; Lambert et al., 2015). In practice, however, it may or may not be feasible to collect data in this manner. If possible, it is recommended that some form of interval recording be collected, at least for a small portion of the day. This will help in the evaluation of the effectiveness of tootling. If this is not possible for some reason (e.g., lack of resources) then data should be collected using one of the other methods discussed in this chapter. The remaining chapters in this book will provide an overview of how Tootling can be implemented in a variety of situations and settings.

References

Alberto, P.A., & Troutman, A.C. (2013). *Applied behavior analysis for teachers* (9th ed.) Pearson Education.

American Psychological Association. (n.d.). Operational definition. In APA dictionary of psychology. Retrieved March, 2022 from https://dictionary.apa.org/operational-definition.

Kazdin, A. E. (1977). Artifact, bias, and complexity of assessment: The ABCs of Reliability. *Journal of Applied Behavior Analysis*, 10(1), 141–150. https://doi.org/10.1901/jaba.1977.10-141.

Lambert, A. M., Tingstrom, D. H., Sterling, H. E., Dufrene, B. A., & Lynne, S. (2015). Effects of tootling on classwide disruptive and appropriate behavior of upper-elementary students. *Behavior Modification*, 39(3), 413–430. https://doi.org/10.1177/0145445514566506.

Lum, J. D. K., Tingstrom, D. H., Dufrene, B. A., Radley, K. C., & Lynne, S. (2017). Effects of tootling on classwide disruptive and academically engaged behavior of general-education high school students. *Psychology in the Schools*, 54(4), 370–384. https://doi.org/10.1002/pits.22002.

Repp, A., Felce, D. & Barton, L. (1988). Basing the treatment of stereotypic and self-injurious behavior on hypotheses and their causes. *Journal of Applied Behavior Analysis*, 21, 281–290.

Richards, S. B., Taylor, R. L., & Ramasamy, R. (2014). Single Subject Research: Applications in Educational and Clinical Settings. *Wadsworth Cengage Learning*.

Part III

Modifications and Evaluation

8 Modifications for Grade Levels

Alexandra Hilt-Panahon and Kennedi Alstead

Modifications for Grade Levels

Up until this point, the previous chapters have focused on creating a deeper understanding of tootling, its components, its effectiveness and the implementation process. However, in order to create a more effective and widely used intervention, it is important to modify the intervention for different populations and settings. It is especially important to adjust interventions based on the age of the population due to some interventions not being developmentally appropriate for certain age groups.

The next three chapters of this book will discuss modifications of tootling for different grade levels, special education classrooms, and non-academic settings. The goal of these three modification chapters is to assist the reader in implementing tootling the most successful way possible for their unique population and to help tailor the intervention to fit their specific needs.

This chapter will focus on modifications to tootling for different grade levels, specifically lower elementary school, upper elementary, middle school, high school, and post-secondary. Previous chapters have referenced studies that have conducted tootling in these settings, and in order to allow for an explanation for recommended modifications, specific studies within each grade level have been selected and will be used as case studies to discuss further modifications that can be made while implementing tootling at different grade levels.

Lower Elementary Modifications

The first set of tootling modifications that can be made is for lower elementary students, also known as the primary grade levels, which typically includes grade K-2 grade. Since tootling is an intervention that includes reading, writing, and understanding of positive behavior, several aspects will need to be modified for the earlier grade levels. Although implementing this intervention in lower grade levels may be more difficult, it is still useful for these students to be trained in an intervention that increases their positive reports of peers as opposed to those negative reports that are commonly seen starting at a young age. The first modification that may be necessary for the primary grade level

DOI: 10.4324/9781003128663-11

students is understanding the students' reading and writing level. This is immensely important as tootling involves reading the "who," "what," and "who reported" with blank areas for the student to fill in the description of the tootle. For students who are just starting to learn and improve their skills in these areas, the original way of writing a tootle may not be sufficient or effective. There are several modifications that could be made in substitution of the original model. These modifications are as follows:

- *Student orally report tootles to the teacher.* This cuts out the writing and reading aspects of the tootling intervention that may decrease its effectiveness for the younger students. The teacher could set up a specific time during the day where students are able to "tootle" to the teacher. Creating a specific time to do this will cut out the distraction or disruption of class time.
- *Create tootle cards with checkboxes for student names and prosocial behavior.* Using checkboxes on a tootle card removes the challenges of the writing portion of the tootling process. This may be a better option for 1st and 2nd grade students who have already developed improved reading skills but their writing skills may not be fully developed for what is required within a typical tootle card.
- *Use pictures to represent prosocial behavior options.* To take the previous modification even further, the prosocial behavior aspect of the tootling card could contain pictures of the behavior instead of listing out the prosocial behavior for an easier way of identifying the behavior conducted by peers.
- *Modifying explanations of prosocial behaviors.* Another aspect of tootling to keep in mind for possible modifications is the understanding of prosocial behavior. Younger students may have a difficult time of understanding the idea of prosocial behavior unless described in terms they are used to hearing. For example, putting it into terms of "sharing with another student," or "helping another student with an answer" may increase their understanding of prosocial behavior.
- *Modifying training sessions.* Increasing the amount of training sessions with shorter times within each training session, and including more interactive training sessions may also help with this.
- *Lower class goal.* When determining the number of tootles needed to receive the class reward, it may be helpful to lower that expectation for the younger students due to the amount of effort required for these students to complete a tootle. Additionally, in order for younger student so continue to be motivated to engage in the intervention, a more immediate reinforcement is preferred.
- *Type of public posting of feedback.* For those younger students, the typical thermometer with increasing numbers toward the overall class goal may be useful; however, if the students are much younger and are still learning their numbers, their progress could be indicated through something simpler (i.e., marking progress through coloring circles in to represent numbers or creating a paper ring train to post around the classroom).

Case Study Example

Cashwell et al. (2001) implemented tootling with second-grade students. The initial tootling study was conducted with fourth-grade students, so these researchers wanted to duplicate the study with younger students to determine if they could be taught to observe and report their peers' prosocial behaviors. The researchers led two, 20-minute group instruction sessions designed to teach students to report their peers' prosocial behaviors. Throughout these training sessions, students were encouraged to define and give examples of prosocial or "helpful" behaviors. The trainer provided an explanation of certain desired prosocial behaviors to report, as well as examples that fit the "helpful" behavior criteria and those that do not fit. Students were then asked to do the same and the trainers provided feedback on their responses. At the end of the first session, the trainers provided the instructions on how to write tootles and students were given time to practice, with feedback provided. The second training session consisted of review of the first session and the experimenter chose the reward for the students for when they reach their goal. The students within this study still used the typical 4 x 6-inch index cards to record their tootles. The tootle box used was a gift-wrapped shoe box that was kept on the teacher's desk and the public posting of their progress toward their goal was indicated through a ladder with a smiley face to depict their total number of tootles.

Upper Elementary Modifications

The next grade level that should be discussed in terms of tootling modifications is upper elementary, which typically contains 3rd through 5th grade students. However, most of the research conducted on tootling has been implemented within these grade levels and has already been adapted to the developmental level of these students. In Chapter 6, How to Implement Tootling, readers have learned how to implement tootling with this age group. Training sessions can include either one or two training sessions with interactive training. The tootle cards can use fill in the blanks for the individual who engaged in the prosocial behavior, what the prosocial behavior was and who wrote the tootle. Additionally, students and teachers should agree on the most desired rewards based on recommendations from students. As always, the teacher can determine what may work best for his/her classroom, but most of the original components of tootling will be effective for upper elementary students.

Middle School Modifications

As we make our way into middle school classrooms, there are several key factors to keep in mind regarding the organization of typical middle schools and the developmental level of middle school students.

- *Understanding the best implementation schedule.* Middle school students are more likely to move between different classrooms and different teachers throughout the day. Therefore, tootling would either need to be introduced and implemented throughout all classrooms for continuity or one specific classroom that has been identified as needing additional behavioral management strategies.
- *Changing the intervention name.* The name "tootling" may not be as appealing for students at this age level or may be distracting to the actual purpose of the intervention. Keeping this in mind when selecting and introducing the intervention is important. Common name changes could include referring it to a competition or a new challenge for their classroom. Tootle cards could be referred to as positive reports or another term that is voted on by the students.
- *Usefulness of oral praise and feedback.* Teachers and school staff should determine if they want to read the written tootles out loud to the classroom. It is common for students at this age to be more focused on peer acceptance, and there is the possibility of students being embarrassed by tootles being read aloud or to be less reinforced by this component.
- *Reward modifications.* Different types of rewards may be more reinforcing to middle school students than elementary students. Teachers may consider incorporating extra credit or no homework for a day for reaching their class goal instead. However, students and teachers can still work together to select the class reward.
- *Determining an effective goal.* Depending on the opportunity within a given class period, a well-thought-out initial goal is important to identify. If the class period is mostly teacher-led instruction with minimal work time, then a smaller goal may be more beneficial to the students initially due to having less time to write a tootle. On the other hand, if there are a lot of opportunities for work time (i.e., independent or with groups), then a larger goal may be up for discussion due to the increase in time available to write a tootle.

Case Study Example

Chaffee et al. (2020) conducted a tootling study with two middle school classrooms. The middle school used a rotating schedule and had 42–49-minute blocks within one school day. The two teachers had requested help from the school psychologist with disruptive student behaviors in their classrooms. Therefore, they used the referral option for selecting classrooms for implementing the tootling intervention. The first class was a 6th grade, general education, English/Language Arts classroom and the second class was a 6th grade, general education, inclusion social studies classroom. Instead of the typical explanation and training of students in tootling, the interventionists and teachers described tootling as a competition. The students also voted on a new name for the intervention, which they ended up calling the positive peer report "positive comments" rather than tootles. The students and teachers agreed on the class-wide reward which was recess. One of the complications the researchers noticed was the students trying to outsmart the intervention (i.e., trying to write as many tootles per day without noticing the behavior). The researchers had to select a cut-off of how many tootles were allowed per day to help with this issue, as well as ignoring the tootles that were jokes or inappropriate.

High School Modifications

Similar to middle schools, the organization and function of the high school setting may affect the implementation of tootling. Several of these modifications will be similar to the middle school setting; however, there may be some key differences discussed between the two.

- *Understanding the best implementation schedule.* Once again, determining which classes to implement tootling can either be done through the implementation across many classes in a specific grade level or through teacher referrals of which classes need additional behavior management support. The second option will often be the most feasible for teachers and other school personnel due to the continued decrease in teachers spent with the same students the older the students get.
- *Changing the intervention name.* Changing the name of tootling will increase the buy-in from staff and students within the high school setting. A name that is more mature or describing the intervention as a competition may be the best option for successful implementation.
- *Usefulness of oral praise and feedback.* It may be helpful to read the classroom dynamic to feel out if reading tootles aloud would increase effectiveness of the intervention or decrease the effectiveness due to students being called out in front of their peers. Peer acceptance is very important during this stage and students may not prefer to be singled out in front of their peers.
- *Reward modifications.* Rewards to classrooms when students reach their goal may also be different. Reinforcing rewards for high school students could be extra credit points, bonus points on tests, or free homework passes.
- *Gauging buy-in from school staff.* Another key factor to consider when implementing tootling in the high school setting is the buy-in from these specific teachers. Many times, high school teachers' time is taken up through their subject taught and it be difficult for them to buy-in to a behavioral intervention that was originally designed for upper elementary students. Figuring out how to modify this intervention and appeal to your audience is extremely important. However, tootling has shown to be effective within the high school setting with specific modifications which will be discussed within this section.
- *Type of public posting of feedback.* In order to implement a developmentally appropriate intervention for high school students, modifications to the

public posting component may be necessary. Something as simple as tally marks in the corner of the white board may be sufficient for these students without the purchasing of a dry-erase thermometer. The teacher can also provide an opportunity for the students to suggest ways to keep track of their progress toward their goal.

- *Determining an effective goal.* Similar to a middle school setting, the layout of a given class period will affect the number of tootles required to reach a class goal. Depending on the opportunity within the class period, a well-thought-out initial goal is important to identify. If the class period is mostly teacher-led instruction with minimal work time, then a smaller goal may be more beneficial to the students initially due to less time to write a tootle. On the other hand, if there are a lot of opportunities for work time (i.e., independent or with groups), then a larger goal may be up for discussion due to the increase in time available to write a tootle.

Case Study Example

The first authors to dive deeper into the tootling research with high school students were Lum et al. (2017). Additionally, two years later, Lum et al. (2019) extended the tootling research within the high school setting. In their first study, tootling was implemented in three general education high school classrooms. This specific high school had four, 95-minute blocks during the school day, for reference. The three classrooms were recruited for the study based on referrals from school administrators for classrooms displaying high levels of disruptive behavior. The three classrooms were an English literature course, a geometry course, and a physical science course. The tootling slips were the same as previous studies, with designated areas to mark "who" and "did" when reporting a tootle. These students, when they reached their goal, were allowed to choose rewards from a predetermined list. The items on the list were free homework passes, bonus points for tests, watching a movie, and edibles (i.e., candy or cookies). The training for these students were similar to other studies; however, the trainers called tootling, "positive comments" and described it as a competition initially. Later, the students were allowed to choose their own name for tootling which varied per classroom based on the most votes.

Within the second study conducted by Lum et al. (2019), most aspects of tootling were similar to their previous study; however, the group contingency was different. Instead of an interdependent group-oriented contingency as seen in most tootling studies, these authors rewarded individual students randomly, known as a randomized independent contingency program. Specifically, two randomly selected student who submitted a tootle received a reward and three students who had a tootle written about them were randomly selected to choose a reward as well. Using this type of contingency system reduced the number of steps the teachers needed to complete each day compared with more traditional forms of tootling. It also resulted in 100%

treatment integrity by the teachers involved in the study. Knowing that both types of contingency programs have demonstrated effectiveness within the high school setting allows practitioners to choose whichever one they deem would be the most effective and feasible for their classroom. Although it is important to keep in mind that the interdependent group-oriented contingency within tootling has more studies that have demonstrated its effectiveness than the independent contingency.

Post-Secondary Modifications

As with the other upper-level grade levels, post-secondary settings may require quite a few modifications in order for the intervention to be successful. There has only been one study conducted that focused on post-secondary students, specifically students with intellectual disabilities (Lipscomb et al., 2018).

- *Determining the need.* The first thing that would be helpful to consider is the type of post-secondary setting that would be necessary to use a positive peer reporting intervention. Most college classes may not have issues with a disruptive classroom environment or maybe it is not relevant for students to report on their peers' positive behaviors. However, those classes that require a lot of group work, smaller class sizes, or a considerable amount of disruptive behavior/lack of academic engagement may benefit from tootling. Additionally, many colleges are now including some sort of inclusive program for students with disabilities, and this could be very helpful for these students as well.
- *Changing the intervention name.* Similar to the middle level and high school level modifications, tootling within a post-secondary setting will most likely require a name change in order for the name to not be too distracting to the students. Students can collectively decide on a name or the professor/educator can decide before introducing it to the students.
- *Reward modifications.* Another adjustment that may be necessary is the type of reinforcement for students to receive once they reach a goal (i.e., extra credit, no homework for the week, etc.).
- *How tootles are reported/recorded.* The way tootles are reported/written may also need to be adjusted in order to make it more college-level appropriate. Assuming most assignments and projects are turned in online or through email, students could report their tootles via email to their professor or some sort of discussion feed using an online program. When Lipscomb et al. (2018) implemented tootling with their students who have intellectual disabilities, they used an online program called ClassDojo that is most commonly used in elementary levels for classroom management purposes. Finding the most appropriate way for the students to report their tootles is extremely important for successful implementation and positive results.
- *Type of public posting of feedback.* Due to the majority of assignments being submitted via an online format, this may be the best way to keep track of

the students' progress toward their class goal. If the tootles are submitted through an online discussion format, then the total number of discussion posts will determine their progress toward their goal. Another option is for the professor to mention their total amount of tootles at the beginning of each class period as part of their PowerPoint presentation before getting into the content of the day.

- *Determining an effective goal.* Similar to determining the need for the intervention, determining an effective goal will also depend on how the class is organized. If tootling is implemented within a college-level classroom with the majority of the class being discussion-focused, then maybe a higher goal is more effective. However, the opposite is also true. If the class is mostly whole-class instruction, then a smaller initial goal may be best.

Case Study Example

For a better understanding on how to implement tootling within a post-secondary setting, specifically within a program for students with disabilities, the study conducted by Lipscomb et al. (2018) will be reviewed. These researchers implemented tootling in a full-emersion experience for adults with disabilities. These students were enrolled in the program, live on campus, and participate in targeted coursework on life-skills, social skills, relationships, employments, community access, as well as typical university courses that may be of interest to the students. At the time of the study, there were a total of 18 students enrolled in the program; however, only the seven students who were freshmen were targeted for this study. The goal of this study was to evaluate the effects of ClassDojo alone and Tootling with ClassDojo in decreasing problem behavior in the classroom. ClassDojo is a free, online behavior management system that allows teachers to track and monitor students' behaviors in class while providing real-time feedback. When ClassDojo and Tootling were conducted together, the instructor reviewed the rules and instructed students to pay close attention to their peers' appropriate behaviors. Students were able to tootle through the use of ClassDojo at designated computers at the end of the class period. To tootle, the student selected the name of the person they wanted to tootle on and select the type of behavior they witnessed from a list of available choices. The results were then visible for all students to see what behaviors they were rewarded for using ClassDojo. The students received a reward if they reached 30 points as a whole class. For this specific study, it was found that ClassDojo alone was more effective than ClassDojo plus tootling. However, it is important for additional studies to be conducted using similar methods.

Summary

For every intervention, it is important to consider modifications or adaptions in order for it to be more effective for the specific population it will be used with. If tootling is to be used with students other than upper elementary students, it may be relevant to consider some of the common modifications listed above. First, developmental level or academic level (i.e., reading or writing performance) should be taken into account due to the expectation of writing a tootle ticket when students notice positive behavior from their peers. If academic performance or developmental level is lower, accommodations to the tootle ticket are needed in order to make the intervention more applicable to the students. In contrast, if students are older, some other form of recording a tootle may be more beneficial, such as using an online program. Second, the name of tootling may need to be adjusted depending on the maturity level of the students. For middle, high school, and post-secondary students, the name "tootling" may be considered too immature and may distract from the purpose of the intervention. Third, the reinforcement should be adjusted based on the grade level or developmental level of the students. Some types of rewards may be more reinforcing for younger students compared to older students and vice versa. Fourth, determining age-appropriate ways to publicly post the class's progress toward reaching their goal is important. Some students may require a more detailed visual of their progress, whereas for other students, a simple tally mark toward their total goal will suffice. Finally, the initial class-wide goal will depend on the age of the students, layout of the class period, and opportunities to write tootles. As time progresses, this goal can increase, but selecting an achievable initial goal is very important for the overall effectiveness of the intervention.

As well different grade levels, considerations will need to be made when implementing tootling within a special education classroom versus a general education classroom. The following chapter will discuss, in a similar format, modifications to successfully implement tootling within a special education classroom setting and alternative education settings. Although there is limited research on tootling for students with disabilities and in other settings that are not the classroom, the authors will use past research to defend the reasoning behind the suggested modifications.

References

Cashwell, T. H., Skinner, C. H., & Smith, E. S. (2001). Increasing second-grade students' reports of peers' prosocial behaviors via direct instruction, group reinforcement, and progress feedback: A replication and extension. *Education & Treatment of Children*, 24(2), 161–175. https://www.jstor.org/stable/42899652.

Chaffee, R. K., Briesch, A. M., Volpe, R. J., Johnson, A. H., & Dudley, L. (2020). Effects of a class-wide positive peer reporting intervention on middle school student behavior. *Behavioral Disorders*, 45(4), 224–237. https://doi.org/10.1177/0198742919881112.

Lipscomb, A. H., Anderson, M., & Gadke, D. L. (2018). Comparing the effects of ClassDojo with and without Tootling intervention in a postsecondary special education classroom setting. *Psychology in the Schools*, 55(10), 1287–1301. https://doi.org/10.1002/pits.22185.

Lum, J. D. K., Radley, K. C., Tingstrom, D. H., Dufrene, B. A., Olmi, D. J., & Wright, S. J. (2019). Tootling with a randomized independent group contingency to improve high school classwide behavior. *Journal of Positive Behavior Interventions*, 21(2), 93–105. https://doi.org/10.1177/1098300718792663.

Lum, J. D. K., Tingstrom, D. H., Dufrene, B. A., Radley, K. C., & Lynne, S. (2017). Effects of tootling on classwide disruptive and academically engaged behavior of general-education high school students. *Psychology in the Schools*, 54(4), 370–384. https://doi.org/10.1002/pits.22002.

9 Modifications for Special Education Classrooms and Alternative Settings

Alexandra Hilt-Panahon, Kennedi Alstead and Lauren Arbolino

The tootling intervention has been studied and shown to be effective in general education classrooms (see Chapter 2 for a comprehensive review). While there has been little research conducted to date that demonstrates the effectiveness of this intervention in special education settings, there is an abundance of evidence that interventions designed for the general education classroom are effective in the special education settings. We can also look to the literature to provide examples of practices designed for Special Education that are commonly used in general education settings (Weiss, 2013.) This chapter will provide examples of how this intervention can be adapted to meet the needs of students in a special education setting.

There are a variety of ways that the Tootling intervention can be adapted without resulting in diminished integrity. In fact, one of the great things about this intervention is that it is incredibly versatile, so it can be used in a variety of settings for a large range of students. This makes it ideal for a special education setting. Before we can consider what to adapt, we need to look at the main components of the intervention. In the case of tootling, the main components are the goal, the target behavior, the reinforcer, the tootle report (tootle card), and public posting of progress. Any of these can be modified, and in some cases, eliminated in order to best meet the needs of the individuals being targeted.

The Goal

The goal that is set is one of the simplest aspects of the intervention to change. In tootling, the goal is a predetermined number of tootles that the whole class is working to meet in order to earn reinforcement. In general education classrooms, this is typically around 30 tootles to start. Given a common general education classroom this is about one tootle per student in the classroom. This number can then be increased as the students become more comfortable with using tootle cards to report peer behavior, with the goal of students continuing to report positive behaviors after external reinforcers have been removed. Generally, initial criteria for reinforcement can be set in a number of ways. The most effective is to determine the baseline level of the target behavior and set the initial goal slightly *lower* than what is observed without

DOI: 10.4324/9781003128663-12

reinforcement. This may sound counterintuitive, but in fact, setting the goal lower at first helps to ensure that the students can earn the reward. Once they have access to the reinforcer it is more likely that they will work to achieve it again in the future, even with a more rigorous goal. In the case of tootling, you cannot determine the number of tootles written before the intervention begins, but you can take data on the number of prosocial interactions occur in the classroom prior to the start of tootling. This number can be used as a basis for determining the class-wide goal. If it is not possible to collect baseline data, using the average of 1 per student is a good place to start.

Consider the following scenario and determine the initial goal for the class:

> Ms. Jenkins has a self-contained EBD classroom with five students in fourth through sixth grades. The students have responded well to a social skills program that she implemented at the beginning of the school year and have been using those skills during their time in social skills group. Ms. Jenkins would like to implement tootling in the classroom to help the students generalize the use of their social skills across the school day. She has recorded the number of positive social interactions she sees in class each day for a week and has determined that currently the students engage in an average of 17 prosocial behaviors per day.

What should Ms. Jenkins set as the initial goal for this class? There are several ways we can go about deciding what is best in this situation. First, we can look to what is typically done or what has been shown to be effective in the past. In the case of tootling, 30 tootles selected as a goal is a standard place to start. This is appropriate for a general education classroom with an average of 25–30 students. If we consider the situation described above, this seems like a very ambitious goal. While it is important to set goals for students that will push them and motivate them to do their best, it is also crucial that the goal is obtainable in order to allow the students to access reinforcement.

Remember, the reinforcer is a means to an end in a reinforcement-based intervention program. As interventionists, we should work to ensure that the students access the reward as often as possible so that they understand the consequences for good behavior. Often, when reinforcement-based programs are set up, teachers think that they need to make it difficult for a student to earn a reward. The thought is that if the student is going to get something they need to work hard to earn it. But it is important to remember, that our goal in implementing an intervention is not to have students earn rewards, but instead to gain valuable skills that they will hopefully take with them when they leave your classroom. So, the purpose of the reinforcer to make sure that the student is motivated to repeat the behavior (in the case of tootling, pro social behaviors) enough times that they become fluent and incorporate the behavior into their daily routine. When we think about rewards in this way, we see that it is vital that students earn more rewards rather than less. For that reason, it is important to set the initial and all subsequent goals at a level that will motivate the student to engage in the behavior.

So, considering that a goal of 30 tootles is what is typical for a general education class and remembering that we want students to access the reward as often as possible, what should we set the goal for this class? Given that the teacher collected data and found that the class averaged 17 prosocial behaviors per day before intervention, it seems a reasonable goal would be 15 prosocial behaviors. This would be obtainable for students to meet quickly, gain access to reinforcement, and therefore be more motivated to continue to engage in prosocial behaviors.

The Target Behavior

In all research to date, the tootling intervention has targeted prosocial behavior. It seems logical, however, that this could be expanded to include all positive behaviors with similar outcomes. If students identify and acknowledge their peer's positive behaviors (academic, social, or behavior) it is likely that these behaviors will continue in the future. Depending on the needs in the classroom, it may be helpful to target on-task of in seat behaviors, rather than focusing solely on social interactions.

In a recent study by Hilt-Panahon, Alstead, Ray, & Panahon (forthcoming) the tootling intervention was implemented in a level IV EBD classroom in a small Midwestern city. While the teacher initially expressed concerns related to peer interactions, it was determined that targeting on-task behavior as well as positive interaction between peers and staff would be most beneficial to improving the behavior of the students in the class. In addition to targeting prosocial interactions between peers, students were also instructed to report on their peer's on-task and positive social interactions with staff. Results indicated that on-task behavior increased for the class after tootling was implemented. The results of this study suggest that the intervention is effective at addressing additional behaviors beyond social skills.

If targeting behaviors other than prosocial behaviors it is important to be sure that they are easily observed by the other students in the class. Discrete, overt behaviors or behaviors that are long in duration are the best to ensure that students will observe and record tootles for these behaviors. Peers will notice students that are sitting quietly and getting their work done or asking a friend for help. Behaviors that are easy to identify and observe will lead to more tootles being reported. When more tootles are reported the class will meet the goal more quickly and will earn the reward. This will motivate them to work harder to meet the goal again and will allow for the intervention to be faded as quickly as possible (see Chapter 11 for more information of fading).

When choosing behaviors to target, it is important to keep the number of behaviors to a minimum. Having too many targets will make it difficult to track student behavior and evaluate behavior change. Students will remember the behaviors and be more likely to notice them if there are a handful of behaviors rather than a long list of targets to look for and report. Determine which behaviors will be most likely to have an impact on the student or students you are targeting and focus on those to start. Additional behaviors can always be added or substituted at a later point in time if needed.

Identifying the Reinforcer

It is always important to match the reward to the individuals in question in order to motivate the students to the best extent possible. When working with a general education classroom, it is often easy to identify a reinforcer that will please the majority, if not all, students in the class. Unfortunately, students in special education are not always motivated by the same rewards as the majority of students at their age or grade level. For this reason, it is important that you identify specific rewards that will be reinforcing to all students in the class. In some special education classes, asking the students want they want to work for may be all that is needed. The age, functional level, and willingness to be a part of the intervention of the student, will determine how best to identify a reward.

The simplest method of determining a reinforcer for the students is to simply ask them for what they want to work toward. This will work well if your students can easily express what they like, will agree on something, and it will not cause problems if someone does not get what they want. If any of the above conditions may occur, there are other ways to adapt the identification of reinforcers for the group.

If students cannot express their wants verbally, you can provide visual options for the students to choose. Picture cards with possible rewards can be shown to the students and they can pick from the possible choices. Often in special education classrooms it is difficult to get students to agree on one reinforcer. This may be due to students' lack of interest in a wide variety of things which will limit what motivates them to work. It can also be due to particular preferences that are not part of the mainstream. Either of these are easily addressed if recognized and addressed accordingly.

The Report

The way in which students report the tootles is one of the simplest ways to individualize the tootling intervention for the special education classroom. As discussed in Chapter 6, students traditionally report their tootles by writing the behavior of their peer, who where and when it occurred on a sheet of paper. That paper is then placed in a tootle box, and the teacher reads some or all of the submitted tootles during the tootle sharing time. This procedure has a great deal of room for adjustment, depending on the needs of the students in the special education classroom.

The tootle card. The tootle card can be adjusted in a variety of ways to fit the needs of the students in the special education classroom. Some of these adaptations have already been discussed in Chapter 7 related to adaptations for students in various grade levels. The way in which students report their peers' positive behavior is flexible; however, what is important is their willingness and participation. Finding ways that make participation more accessible to all students in the class is a priority. The following section provides examples of ways the tootle card can be modified and for whom it may be appropriate.

Picture cards. The tootle card was originally designed for students to write down the prosocial behaviors that they observed their peers engage in. In order for this to be an effective method, all students participating in the intervention must be able to write legibly, so the tootle can be read by the teacher during sharing time. In addition, students need to know how to spell, at least to a level that someone else can gain meaning from what is written on the card. Finally, all students in the class must be motivated to report the tootles in this way. It may be a challenge to meet all of these criteria in a general education classroom, it may be even more difficult in special education classrooms. One possible solution to these concerns is to provide students with an alternate method for reporting tootles. One of the easiest ways to do this is to provide picture-based tootle cards. These cards provide students with a picture that they can use to indicate peer behavior. The students are provided with pictures of typical classroom behaviors that they can circle if they see a peer engage in any of the behaviors listed. This card could also be adapted to include pictures of classmates in order to help students to easily identify the correct peer. This type of tootle card would be ideal for students in the lower grades and/or students who cannot read. This could be adopted class-wide, or provided to specific students as needed.

In this example, the students in the class are listed in one column and common prosocial classroom behaviors are listed in a separate column. Boxes are provided next to each name and behavior so that students can check off the appropriate student and behavior. While this version requires students to be able to read, it allows them to participate without having to write. Many students in special education have difficulty with writing, and may be unwilling or unable to participate in order to avoid having to write. By alleviating that barrier, students may be more likely to take part in the intervention.

Table 9.1 Modified Tootle Card

Who	Did what:	For whom:
☐ Grayden	☐ answered a question	☐ Grayden
☐ Eric	☐ shared	☐ Eric
☐ Patrick	☐ gave a compliment	☐ Patrick
☐ Johnnie	☐ worked together	☐ Johnnie
☐ Ian	☐ helped	☐ Ian
	☐ played together	☐ Staff
	☐ was kind	
	☐ Other: _____	

Another way to report tootles would be to have students verbally report their tootles through audio or video recording. This would be a novel way for them to capture the tootle while also making it fun and interesting for the student. In order to do this, there needs to be a designated area in the classroom that students can go to record the tootle. Students should be taught what to report (peer, positive behavior, and who is reporting the tootle), as well as how to use the recording device and when it is appropriate to record tootles. In some classrooms it may be possible to have students record any time they see a positive behavior. For others, it may be better to have students wait for specific times.

Finally, for students who can't or won't complete a tootle on their own, the teacher or aides in the classroom can help them. Students can dictate the tootle to an adult who can record it for the student. Students may be more willing to report tootles if there is less required of them to do so. This can be extremely important to consider in special education classrooms where students may struggle with reading and writing to a greater degree than in a general education classroom.

The Public Posting of Progress

Public posting of progress has been shown to motivate students and increase gains (Van Houten & Van Houten, 1977). Public posting is an important component of the tootling intervention, as it allows all students to be aware of the progress toward the group goal. Public posting takes many forms, from names on a chalk board to computer programs that track student performance. In the tootling intervention, the number of tootles is tracked and publicly posted in order to allow students to know how close the group is to its goal.

The group goal can be posted in a variety of ways in the classroom. Depending on the population of students in the class, the way in which progress is posted can be important to the success of the intervention. The simplest way to display the number of tootles earned is to post the number of tootles reported somewhere in the room. This could be written on the chalkboard or posted on a bulletin board. For many students this will be enough to provide the information students need to know how close they are to receiving reinforcement. For many students in special education, however, there may be other ways to support students in working toward the group goal.

One way to increase student understanding of their progress toward the goal is to provide a visual demonstration of just how close or far from the goal the students are. By showing students their progress in a concrete way, it allows for better understanding of what more needs to done to meet the goal. Some examples of how to provide students with a visual are listed below. Regardless of how it is displayed, the important thing is that the students can visualize both how many tootles have been recorded and how many are still needed to meet the goal.

A simple visual to use is a thermometer. To do this, the teacher writes the goal at the top of the thermometer and tick marks for numbers leading up to the goal. Each day, after sharing tootles students have submitted, the teacher (or a student) should add up the tootles and color in that amount on the thermometer. This is repeated daily until the class makes their goal. Once the goal has been reached, the class earns the reward and the process starts over.

This idea of a thermometer can be adapted in many ways to suit the needs and preferences of students in a class. It is a good idea to incorporate student preferences into the intervention whenever possible. The thermometer idea could be adapted to incorporate a variety of themes and interests. For example, instead of a thermometer, it could be set up as a racetrack if students like cars, a football field for sports fans, or an animal race for animal lovers. Again, the method of posting is not important. What is important is that the students are able to see their progress and keep track of it.

Tootling with Students with Behavior Difficulties

Tootling has been shown to be effective in decreasing disruptive behaviors and increasing prosocial behaviors of students in a relatively narrow sample of students within the general education classroom; therefore, it is important for research to demonstrate the effectiveness of tootling with other student populations within the school system, such as students with Emotional Behavioral Disorders (EBD). The number of students with EBD is increasing in the early elementary classrooms (Niesyn, 2009). Students that are receiving special education services, especially those served under the EBD category, are more likely to exhibit problem behaviors and a lack of strong social skills, which subjects them to teasing and bullying (Margraf & Pinquirt, 2016). These students are more likely to be grouped together in more restrictive placements than the general education classroom (Hofstadter et al., 2009). Students with EBD may be more likely to believe that rule breaking behavior helps with peer acceptance and have poor peer relationships.

Strengthening the prosocial behaviors of students with EBD while decreasing their disruptive behaviors may help to improve their quality of social interactions and decrease the instances of social rejection (Margraf & Pinquirt, 2016). In addition, it is beneficial to increase positive peer relations for students with EBD because the placement of all students in a self-contained classroom can increase the disruptions and interfere with the learning environment (Hofstadter et al., 2009). There has been an increasing trend in using positive behavioral interventions with students with challenging behaviors (Conroy et al., 2005). Providing special education teachers with these positive behavioral interventions as well as classroom management skills can be very helpful for the teachers and their students. Overall, special education teacher preparation, strong classroom organization, and behavior management skills are extremely important for teachers of students with EBD (Oliver & Reschly, 2010).

Modifications for Non-Academic Settings

Historically, Positive Peer Reporting and Tootling were conducted in educational settings. Originally, the intent of the intervention was to encourage positive peer responding through encouragement fostered in a classroom environment. Other students and a teacher are integral pieces of making this concept work. Fewer studies have examined the use of Positive Peer Reporting and Tootling in non-educational settings. However, the idea of encouraging positive peer responding could theoretically occur any place where there is more than one peer present and an adult. If we are able to generalize the intervention to different settings where groups of children are together with an adult, we could implement Positive Peer Reporting and Tootling to achieve positive outcomes.

Students who engage in repeated negative behaviors such as provoking others and being uncooperative with peers are at risk for poor social relationships with peers, social rejection, decreased academic functioning, and other negative academic and social outcomes. Dealing with repeated negative behaviors can become time consuming and frustrating, takes time away from instruction and other classroom activities, and can lead to a negative classroom environment. Positive Peer Reporting (PPR) and Tootling are designed to target specific students who are at risk for social rejection due to their negative interactions with other students. PPR provides incentive for students to engage in positive behaviors and focus on positive behaviors displayed by their peers through daily compliments sessions. During each compliment session, specific students are praised by their peers for displaying positive, prosocial behaviors throughout the day. PPR is effective in improving social interactions, peer acceptance, and social involvement across settings and ages and creates a more positive classroom environment. There are several components that distinguish PPR from Tootling. During PPR, children publicly report prosocial behaviors. During Tootling, prosocial behaviors are reported privately and anonymously. PPR usually is limited to specific times of the day, whereas Tootling can take place anytime. Traditionally, PPR has been used to improve the social interactions of individuals; Tootling has been used to improve the social interactions of a group.

If nonpreferred behaviors for attention are happening for children in the school environment, it is reasonable to extend that these same children are searching for attention by any means that are accessible, easy, convenient, and fast outside of the school environment as well. PPR and Tootling are just as important in non-school settings. In 1976, Grieger et al. published the first of many studies looking at the effectiveness of an intervention designed to decrease antisocial behavior in children by reinforcing peers' reports of classmates' prosocial behaviors. They found that rewarding Kindergarteners (n=90) for naming a peer who had done something nice resulted in increased observed cooperative play and decreased aggression. Two decades later, Ervin et al. (1996) described a similar intervention designed for use in a Boys Town residential treatment center for youth. Their idea was motivated by author Ken Kesey's theory that socially ostracized individuals could be aided through targeted positive attention. Ervin et al. (1996) were the first authors to coin the term "positive peer reports" to describe their method of rewarding children for praising one another.

Benefits of PPR/Tootling in Alternative Settings

Many children who are in alternative or clinical settings could benefit from examples for appropriate and positive social interaction. Children and adolescents can show deficits in social skills due to a myriad of factors. These weaknesses change and may become more apparent as children age and social navigations of surroundings become more complex. It is critical that children learn how to navigate their environments. Social Skills Training refers to a wide range of interventions and instructional methods used to help an individual understand and improve social skills. Sometimes referred to as social skills groups, the training is often associated with the fields of applied behavior analysis, special education, cognitive-behavioral therapy, and relationship-based therapies. A variety of professionals work with students on improving social skills, including teachers, behavior analysts, psychologists, therapists, and more. It has also been demonstrated that parents can train to implement social skills programs effectively.

Social skills groups in clinical settings are common and are becoming more available in hospital, private and community-based settings. Weak social skills in children are common and can be found in children diagnosed with Attention-Deficit Hyperactivity Disorder (ADHD), Autism Spectrum Disorder (ASD). Non-Verbal Learning Disorder (NVLD), and Social Communication Disorder (SCD) to name a few. Environmental factors, learning history, anxiety, or depression can also play a role for some children in poor or stunted social skill development. Skills these children learn in a clinical setting can maintain and have the possibility of generalizing to other areas in their life.

For children who are used to getting into trouble or have rarely been in situations where they get praised, continuous praise help improve their overall self-esteem. This contributes to positive therapeutic outcomes. Positive self-concept allows children to create and maintain healthy and satisfying relationships. Self-concept aids in knowing what to say in specific situations, how to make good decisions and how to effectively manage different social situations without as much reticence. These skills can be practiced and strengthened in clinical settings.

Positive praise and improved self-esteem also demonstrate decreased anxiety and decreased depressive symptoms. Self-esteem has been linked to anxiety, depression, academic progress and stress. Self-esteem has been documented as having a significant effect on physical and emotional health and social outcomes during childhood and adolescence. Academic achievement, occupational success, better social relationships, a sense of well-being, good coping skills and motivation have connection to positive self-esteem. Low self-esteem is related to depression, stress, substance abuse, suicidal ideation, and poor functioning.

Research has shown that praise is contagious. Children can benefit from spreading positivity to others. Historically, research has demonstrated there is a tendency for humans to imitate other people's emotional expressions automatically or unconsciously. Exposure to another's emotion in a social situation can even lead to the belief in those specific and unique emotions and the response to take them on as our own, just through exposure to that emotion. Emotional contagion (EC) is the process through which a person or group influences the emotions and affective behavior of another person or a group. Sigal Barsade (2002) has found in his research outcomes revealing that those affected by positive emotional contagion experienced improved cooperation, decreased conflict and increased task performance.

Ownership and Independence

Students become agents of their own change, which is empowering and leads to accountability and increased motivation to continue with progress they are making. Positive Peer Reporting and Tootling create a process in which children are actively creating positive change for themselves. Thus, it is helping them become problem solvers. This contributes to helping children identify problems, think about solutions, analyze solutions and then trying to see what may work. As they get older the skills to speak with a teacher about a missed assignment or the doctor about why they don't feel well will be easier if children see themselves as capable change agents. The ability to recognize and confront problems will be a life skill that can be practiced.

Anxiety has always been a concern for adolescent mental health. Since the beginning of the COVID-19 pandemic, a recent meta-analysis demonstrated a clinically significant increase in adolescent anxiety. The coronavirus (COVID-19) pandemic has disrupted the lives of individuals around the world. In the U.S., city and state-wide shelter-in-place orders were implemented across the country as early as March 2020. This forced most Americans to adjust to new circumstances (e.g., studying and working from home), take on new roles (e.g., caretaker, teacher), and deal with new or exacerbated hardship (e.g., job loss, reduced income, illness, social isolation, and restricted mobility). The nature and full extent of the impact of COVID-19 is only beginning to be understood as this unprecedented crisis unfolds.

Obstacles to Positive Peer Reporting/Tootling

Many factors can contribute to the difficulty of implementing PPR/Tootling in a noneducational setting. First, it is more likely to find professionals who are poorly trained or never exposed to those concepts and resources (such as Applied Behavior Analysis or Positive Behavioral Intervention Supports) outside of the school setting. This can contribute to the difficulty of buy-in and the likely resistance to learning about, implementing, and then continuing with approaches rooted in these beliefs. It may be difficult to be consistent and provide high fidelity of the intervention due to shortages of staff or number of adults involved. Another concern with implementation outside of the school setting is that the isolated child feels stigmatized. Even children who thrive on peer attention may feel uncomfortable about having their name appear on the list of children to receive compliments.

Children may disguise unfriendly remarks as "compliments". As with any other intervention strategy, children may initially "test the limits" with Positive Peer Reporting. Sometimes they may make cutting comments about others under the guise of complimenting them (e.g., "I want to praise Sally for taking a bath today"). Children offer only vague praise.

Addressing Obstacles

Several tactics can be used to combat obstacles. Providing online training that is accessible to a wider group of people. Providing virtual boosters/support to increase level of consistency. Consider having some children as the target for compliments less than daily. If you find that a child is attempting to undermine the program, meet with him or her in private. Share your concern that the behavior is contributing to a negative atmosphere and that isn't the goal of the program. If the child persists in making hurtful comments after your conference, avoid calling on that person to give praise and be sure to enforce appropriate consequences for any negative remarks.

If they seem to struggle to give specific or meaningful praise, model for them. For instance, if a child says of a peer, "Joe looked like he was paying attention to what we were doing today", you might follow up with more specific praise: "Yes, that's right. In fact, Joe asked several good questions that got everybody talking about the topic. That's the kind of participation that gets us involved in learning!" Also, don't be shy about letting children know when they have praised well. If you highlight and discuss positive comments that you believe are terrific examples of praise, you can help others to develop standards of quality for judging compliments.

Examples

Use Positive Peer Reporting to Improve Group Climate. As a clinician, you may want to adopt the Positive Peer Reporting strategy for a group even if you do not have children who regularly seek negative attention. All children can benefit from the chance to practice giving and receiving compliments. You may also find that, once the intervention is in place, your children begin to be more complimentary toward one another and use fewer putdowns.

Extend Positive Peer Reporting to Less Structured Situations. Once this strategy is in place and effective, you can experiment with extending it to situations in which there is less structure and direct adult supervision (generalization). You may announce, for example, that children can earn a certain number of additional bonus points for each sincere compliment that another adult in their lives observes being used in another setting. You can make this generalization strategy more effective by sharing specific instances in which you heard that a child was giving praise or compliments (e.g., "I am giving a point to our group because, on the playground yesterday with his family, Jacob's mom heard him teaching some of the younger kids how to play freeze tag. He also complimented them on how quickly they learned the rule. I bet it made them feel good to have an older child pay that kind of attention to them"). Historically, Positive Peer Reporting and Tootling were conducted in educational settings. Originally, the intent of the intervention was to encourage positive peer responding through encouragement fostered in a classroom environment. Other students and a teacher are integral pieces of making this concept work. Fewer studies have examined the use of Positive Peer Reporting and Tootling in non-educational settings. However, the idea of encouraging positive peer responding could theoretically occur any place where there is more than one peer present and an adult. If we are able to generalize the intervention to different settings where groups of children are together with an adult, we could implement Positive Peer Reporting and Tootling to achieve positive outcomes.

References

Barsade, S. G. (2002). The Ripple Effect: Emotional Cognition and Its Influence on Group Behavior. *Administrative Science Quarterly*, 47, 644–675.

Bowers, F. E., McGinnis, C., Ervin, R. A., & Friman, P. C. (1999). Merging research and practice: The example of positive peer reporting applied to social rejection. *Education and Treatment of Children*, 22, 218–226.

Bowers, F. E., Woods, D. W., Carlyon, W. D., & Friman, P. C. (2000). Using positive peer reporting to improve the social interactions and acceptance of socially isolated adolescents in residential care: A systematic replication. *Journal of Applied Behavioral Analysis*, 33, 239–242.

Conroy, M. A., Dunlap, G., Clarke, S., & Alter, P. J. (2005). A descriptive analysis of positive behavioral intervention research with young children with challenging behaviors. *Topics in Early Childhood Special Education*, 25(3), 157–166. https://doi.org/10.1177/02711214050250030301.

Ervin, R. A., Miller, P. M., & Friman, P. C. (1996). Feed the hungry bee: Using positive peer reports to improve the social interactions and acceptance of a socially rejected girl in residential care. *Journal of Applied Behavior Analysis*, 29(2), 251–253. https://doi.org/10.1901/jaba.1996.29-251.

Grieger, T., Kauffman, J. M., & Grieger, R. M. (1976). Effects of peer reporting on cooperative play and aggression of kindergarten children. *Journal of School Psychology*, 14(4), 307- 313. https://doi.org/10.1016/0022-4405(76)90027-3.

Hilt-Panahon, A., Alstead, K., Ray, J., & Panahon, C. J. (forthcoming). *The effectiveness of the tootling intervention for students with EBD*.

Hofstadter, K. L., Jones, K. M., & Therrien, W. J. (2009). Classwide effects of positive peer reporting on the on-task behavior of children with emotional disturbance. *Journal of Evidence-Based Practices for Schools*, 10(1), 2–19.

Murphy, J. (2013). Positive peer reporting interventions with high vs. low experimenter-involvement in an alternative education setting. *Dissertations*. https://

www.proquest.com/openview/c62ce1692e8e8e636592bef5938ab831/1?pq-origsite= gscholar&cbl=18750.

Murphy, J., & Zlomke, K. (2014). Positive Peer Reporting in the Classroom: a Review of Intervention Procedures. *Behavior analysis in practice*, 7(2), 126–137. https://doi. org/10.1007/s40617-014-0025-0

Margraf, H., & Pinquirt, M. (2016). Bullying and social support: Variation by school-type and emotional or behavioural disturbances. *Emotional and Behavioural Difficulties*, 21(3), 258–270. https://doi.org/10.1080/13632752.2016.1165970.

Niesyn, M. E. (2009). Strategies for success: Evidence-based instructional practices for students with emotional and behavioral disorders. *Preventing School Failure*, 53(4), 227–233. https://doi.org/10.3200/PSFL.53.4.227-234.

Oliver, R. M., & Reschly, D. J. (2010). Special education teacher preparation in classroom management: Implications for students with emotional and behavioral disorders. *Behavioral Disorders*, 35(3), 188–199. https://doi.org/10.1177/019874291003500301.

Sherman, J. C. (2012). Positive Peer Reporting and Positive Peer Reporting Combined With Tootling: A Comparison of Interventions. *Dissertations*, 857. https://aquila. usm.edu/dissertations/857.

Van Houten, R., & Van Houten, J. (1977). The performance feedback system in the special education classroom: An analysis of public posting and peer comments. *Behavior Therapy*, 8(3), 366–376.

Weiss, S. L. (2013). Learning-Related Behaviors: Small Group Reading Instruction in the General Education Classroom. *Intervention in School and Clinic*, 48(5), 294–302. https://doi. org/10.1177/1053451212472231.

10 Treatment Integrity

Alexandra Hilt-Panahon and Kennedi Alstead

Treatment Integrity

When assessing the effectiveness of any intervention, the first thing that should be evaluated is the integrity with which the intervention is implemented. Intervention Integrity, also referred to as Intervention Fidelity, is defined as "the delivery of an intervention or program as designed" (Gresham et al., 2000; O'Donnell, 2008). In order to maximize the possibility of success, it is important to follow the intervention plan as it was designed in order to ensure it is implemented correctly. Partially implementing an intervention can impact its overall success. Consider the following scenario.

> Your tooth is hurting and has been for several weeks. You can no longer take the pain so you schedule an appointment with your dentist. After a consultation, your dentist tells you that he needs to pull the tooth. On the day of your procedure, the dentist meets with you to go over the plan for extracting the tooth. He provides you with a 10-step process that has been refined over time and demonstrated to be highly effective in safely extracting the tooth and reducing the risk of infection. As he finishes his explanation of the procedures, he tells you that while he knows the protocol is effective, he doesn't complete the eighth step, which is to sanitize the room and mouth prior to starting the operation. He tells you that while he knows it is helpful for some, he finds that it takes a long time to do, patients don't like to have to wait, and no one in his practice has gotten sick.

If you were in this surgeon's office, would you want him to do your surgery? Most people would not think twice about canceling the appointment. Why would someone want to trust a doctor who was not going to follow the procedures necessary on purpose, simply because a step was inconvenient? While this seems absurd, this often happens in educational settings when professionals implement interventions with children. In fact, treatment fidelity is often overlooked when evaluating the impact of interventions in schools (Swanson et al., 2011). While fidelity is highly valued in a medical context, it is

DOI: 10.4324/9781003128663-13

less so when interventions are implemented in school and counseling situations. Some could argue that fidelity is more important in a medical setting due to the impact that medical interventions have on people's health and well-being. While this is true, one could argue that academic and behavioral interventions also have an impact on a person's academic and social emotional health. For this reason, it is imperative that school-based interventions be afforded the same level of attention as it relates to fidelity as a medical intervention.

Treatment integrity is defined as the degree to which a treatment is implemented as planned (Gresham et al., 2017). Integrity, also referred to as treatment fidelity, is a key factor in whether or not an intervention that is implemented will be successful or not. A study conducted by Gresham et al. (2017) evaluated the importance of monitoring integrity. In this study, 181 experimental studies published between 1980 and 1990 were reviewed to determine if integrity was or was not assessed, as well as other critical factors of integrity. Of these many studies, only 14.4% reported integrity data and only 34% (65 studies) operationally defined treatments. This demonstrates that, while important to the success of intervention implementation, treatment integrity is often overlooked.

Researchers have identified multiple components that make up treatment integrity. These include adherence, quality of delivery, program differentiation, exposure, and participant responsiveness (Dane & Schneider, 1998) as well as intervention adaptation (Durlak & DuPre, 2008). These components, described below, can serve to enhance or hinder the integrity of any intervention.

Adherence refers to how closely the interventionist follows the intervention as it was originally developed. This includes completing all components of the intervention in the order and manner that the developer intended. Delivery quality evaluates the interventionist's skills implementing the intervention. Are they able to conduct the intervention easily, and make good decisions using sound judgements. While adherence focuses more on the interventionist's willingness to implement the intervention as intended, quality of delivery refers to their ability to do so. So, someone may want to implement the intervention with perfect integrity, but they do not have the skills, training, or ability to do so. How much the intervention differs from other practices utilized in the environment is referred to as program differentiation and can have an effect on integrity. Often, interventions are not implemented with fidelity due to the intervention differing significantly from typical classroom practices (Dunst & Trivette, 1988). Exposure refers to how much intervention the person receives. Also known as dosage, this takes in to account for how long the intervention is implemented, and the number and duration of sessions. Treatment integrity can also be impacted by the level of engagement of both the student and the interventionist. This is referred to as participant responsiveness.

When evaluating integrity, there are numerous characteristics of all involved that may influence the integrity of an intervention. Roach, Lawton, & Elliott (2014) outlined specific characteristics that may help or hinder the integrity of a given intervention. These include characteristics of the intervention itself, as well as the interventionist and the student or students involved.

Intervention characteristics. Multiple variables related to the intervention may help to increase integrity. These include the acceptability of the intervention, how quickly behavior change is observed, how flexible the intervention is to adapt to different environments, and how compatible it is with practices already in place. Variable that may hinder integrity may be the complexity of the intervention, the amount of resources that are needed for implementation, including money and time. If an intervention is designed to be simple to implement, low in demands of time and resources, and adapts easily to the current environment will be more likely to be successful than if these characteristics are not met.

Interventionist characteristics. Just as with any educational practice, the interventionist has a significant influence over the fidelity of an intervention. The level of training of the individual implementing the intervention may impact fidelity. This may include how well trained they are in relation to the specific intervention as well as training related to education in general. Another factor that will influence the level of integrity is how motivated the interventionist is to use the intervention. This may be influenced by how confident they are in their ability to implement the intervention as well as how strongly they believe that the intervention will work.

Student Characteristics. Finally, Roach and colleagues (2014) outline several variables related to the students themselves that may impact the level of implementation fidelity. First, the student's level of motivation is important. If the students wants to change their behavior, or is excited about the intervention it will be more likely that they will be cooperative. This makes implementation easier and more likely for the interventionist to adhere to the steps of the intervention. Some issues that may hinder implementation include the nature of the student's problem behavior including how long it has been occurring the intensity of the problem behavior. More severe behaviors may make it more difficult to administer interventions.

Ensuring Fidelity

There are several steps that can be taken before the start and during implementation of an intervention in order to guarantee a high level of intervention fidelity. First, it is important to carefully plan your intervention and make sure that everyone involved in its implementation is on the same page related to all aspects of the intervention. Teachers, paras, and all other school personnel that will be involved in tootling should have a clear understanding of what it entails, and the mechanisms that make the intervention effective. This can be accomplished by having all staff educate themselves about tootling prior to starting with students. You are already completing this step by reading this book! After everyone has a good idea of what tootling is and how it is conducted, all professionals should come together to determine how exactly the intervention will be implemented in the designated setting. Decisions that need to be made include what the tootle cards will look like, when students will write and turn in tootles, when the teacher will read the tootles and update the tootle count, how progress will be displayed, how reinforcers will be chosen, and how the team will evaluate the effectiveness of the intervention. Input from the entire team on what and how the intervention will be implemented has been shown in the research to increase the integrity of implementation (Anderson & Daly, 2013). It is vital that there is buy in from all involved in order for everyone to be invested in implementation. If a member of the team does not have confidence in the intervention, or disagrees with the principles used to change behavior,

After implementation decisions are made, team members can be assigned tasks to get everything ready for the start of tootling. Next, training should be planned and scripted to make sure that there is consistency in how it is conducted, especially if the training will occur over multiple days and/or with multiple people. All of these steps will help to ensure that individuals that implement this intervention will do so with consistency and as completely as possible.

In order to ensure that all of the steps are followed, it is helpful to make a checklist that can be filled out as individuals complete each task. So, if we develop a checklist for our Pre-Intervention Tasks, it would look something like this:

Tootling Preparation Checklist

Table 10.1 Tootling Preparation Checklist

Task	Person Responsible	Date Completed (Write date with Initials)	Notes
Step 1: all staff educate themselves about tootling prior to starting with students	All staff		
Step 2: Hold meeting to determine particulars of intervention	All Staff		
Step 3: Complete Individual task			
o Design tootle cards	Sally		
o Write script for tootle meeting	Jen		
o Create tootle board	Bob		
o Purchase clear container for tootles	Maria		
o Collect baseline data	Ben		
o Develop training script	Maria		
Step 4: Conduct training	Maria & Ben		

This preparation checklist should be kept with the leader of the team, most often the classroom teacher. As people complete their tasks they can date and initial their work so that everyone can see as progress is made. If, for some reason, one individual is not able to get things done, that will be seen as well and can be rectified before it is too late. Finally, this guarantees that you will have everything you need and everyone will be ready prior to the start of the intervention. If this step is skipped, it is likely that some aspect of the intervention preparation will be missed and the chances of success are less likely.

Intervention Protocols

Another important component of intervention preparation is developing a protocol for implementation. An Intervention Protocol is defined as a written description of the intervention. It includes the intervention's objectives, the steps for implementation, and how it will be evaluated. Each step of the intervention should be described in enough detail that someone could conduct the intervention based on the description provided. This is crucial for accuracy and consistency of implementation across the course of the intervention. An example of a protocol for the training session discussed above is provided here:

Tootling Student Training Session Protocol

Two 15-minute training sessions. Day One:

- Introduce the tootling procedure as something students will do in class.
- Provide verbal examples of prosocial behaviors.
- Role play examples if students are having a difficult time understanding.
- Ask students to give their own examples of how they help others at home and at school.
- Ask students to provide examples of how they help or be kind to each other.
- Define tattling (telling the teacher when a peer did something wrong) and tootling (telling the teacher when a peer did something helpful or being kind to others).
- Give students examples of tootling (e.g., helping a student pick up their books, loaning a student a pencil, showing a student how to work a math problem).
- Have students provide their own examples.
- Praise examples that fit criteria for tootling; give corrective feedback when students give examples that do not fit the criteria.
- Remind students that we will review this the following day.

Day Two:

- Define tootling as reporting when peers do something helpful or are kind to others.
- Remind students that tootling does not involve reporting their own behaviors, just their classmates' prosocial behaviors.

- Remind students that they are only to report peers for helping classmates, not their teacher or other adults.
- Pass out index cards and have students write down examples of tootling, Who (classmate) did what (helpful behavior), and for whom (who they helped). Students may choose to use "Box check" cards instead of writing.
- Collect examples.
- Read examples aloud and provide praise for examples that fit criteria; corrective feedback for examples that do not fit criteria

As we can see from this example, the protocol outlines each step of the training and who is responsible for what. This then serves as a prompt to those conducting training as well as providing a simple way to review and make sure that the training is being conducted as intended. These protocols can also be saved and used for students in the future that may need the same intervention. This reduces the amount of work for teachers and other school professionals. A protocol should be developed for any intervention, including tootling. Provided below is a generic

Table 10.2 Tootling Protocol

Step in Tootle Intervention	Yes or NO
1. Tootle cards are in the correct position	
2. Tootle cards are visible to students	
3. Tootle box is visible to students	
4. Teacher reads the tootles to the classroom in the morning (including the name of the tootler, prosocial behavior, and who engaged in the behavior)	
5. Teacher provides specific praise to student who wrote the tootle	
6. Teacher provides specific praise to student who received the tootle	
7. Teacher provides corrective feedback when needed (for an incorrect tootle)	
8. Tootle box is visible to students	
9. Tootle goal is/has been set	
10. Class-wide reward is/has been decided	
11. If class reaches their goal, reward is provided	
12. If class reaches their goal, a new goal is set	
13. If class reaches their goal, a new reward is decided	
14. Teacher informs the class of their current number of tootles	
15. Dry-erase thermometer is visible to the students	
16. Range of number of tootles is written on thermometer	
17. Teacher marks the number of tootles collected from the previous day on the thermometer	
18. If the thermometer is full, the thermometer is erased	

example of a tootling protocol. This can and should be adapted to the specific situation in which you are implementing the intervention. The steps should be followed as described below, but can be adapted if necessary to the situation.

The intervention protocol should be used each time the intervention is implemented. Best practice dictates that someone other than the person implementing the intervention should observe and complete the integrity protocol. This is suggested to maintain a level of objectivity in the evaluation of the implementation. It is easier for someone not involved in the intervention to evaluate how well it is implemented. So, if possible, find an impartial observer to watch the intervention and record the steps completed and missed. This could be another teacher, the school psychologist or social worker, or the principal to name a few. While some people may find it intimidating to have someone else watch them, remember that the purpose of collecting fidelity information is to improve how the intervention is conducted. The higher the level of fidelity, the more likely the intervention will be successful and student behavior will improve. If someone watching notices that a step or steps are not being done correctly, this can be very helpful information for you as the intervention agent.

While having an independent observer is ideal, it is not always possible. If another person is not available, it is better to gather the information yourself than not at all. When self-reporting is used, it is best to collect data in the same manner as an independent observer would. So, an integrity checklist should be used and should be completed during the intervention. When collecting self-report data, it is imperative that the interventionist be objective in their assessment of the implementation (Noell, et al., 2005). The purpose of collecting these data is to determine if any improvements can be made, which will likely lead to benefits for students. It is important to remember that the goal of integrity data is to ensure that the intervention will be as effective as possible. If the interventionist isn't accurate in their recording, this will not be possible.

After fidelity data are collected the next step is to evaluate the data to determine if integrity has been established. The question of what level of integrity is considered acceptable has been debated in the literature, but most researchers would agree that integrity above 80% demonstrates a high level of fidelity. In addition, anything below 50% is considered low fidelity. Therefore anything in between 50–79% is considered moderate fidelity (Borrelli, 2005). These guidelines can be very helpful when evaluating an intervention in an applied setting. The follow provides an example of how fidelity data may be used to improve intervention effectiveness.

The Pre-referral intervention team at Albert Elementary decides to start a tootling intervention in a third grade general education classroom. The decision to start the intervention was based on referrals that the classroom teacher, Mr. Hogan, had made to the team related to the students' difficulty interacting positively with each other. The teacher reported that the students know how to be kind, but that they are not to each other. The team works together to develop an intervention protocol. They share this with the teacher, train him on how to use tootling in his classroom, and help with the training for the students. After two weeks of implementation the Mr. Hogan returned to the team meeting to report on progress. He stated that tootling doesn't work and that he would like to try something else. The team decides to come to the classroom to observe the intervention in action before making the decision to abandon tootling entirely. The teacher agrees to try it for one more day and allow Dr. Evans, the school psychologist, to come to class and observe.

The next morning, Dr. Evans arrives to the classroom at the beginning of the school day. She uses the intervention protocol developed by the team as her guide to evaluating the integrity of implementation.

The protocol is provided below.

Table 10.3 Tootling Intervention Protocol

Step	Description	Completed? (Y or N)
1	Welcome students as they enter the classroom	
2	Tell the students it is time for Tootling Review	
3	Ask for examples of behavior that should be reported	
4	Call on at least 3 students for examples – Provide praise if correct – Provide corrective feedback in incorrect	
5	Tell students it is time to review tootles from previous school day	
6	Read a minimum of 3 tootles from previous school day	
7	Provide praise to the student- behavior was reported	
8	Provide praise for the students that tootled	
9	Count the total number of tootles reported on previous school day	
10	Update the Tootle Count	
11	Remind students of reward	
12	If goal was met- – when they will get their If goal not met- – Let students know how many more tootles are needed to earn reward	
		Total:

According to the protocol, Mr. Hogan is supposed to welcome students and start the tootling review from the previous day. After reading a minimum of 3 tootles from the day before, he is to count them all and update the progress chart at the front of the room. If the students meet the goal, Mr. Hogan is then supposed to remind them of the reward and let them know when they will receive it. Dr. Evans observes as Mr. Hogan starts the day and notes the steps to the intervention that are implemented correctly. Here are the results of Dr. Evans observation.

Table 10.4 Tootling Intervention Protocol

Step	Description	Completed? (Y or N)
1	Welcome students as they enter the classroom	Y
2	Tell the students it is time for Tootling Review	Y
3	Ask for examples of behavior that should be reported	N
4	Call on at least 3 students for examples 　－　Provide praise if correct 　－　Provide corrective feedback in incorrect	N
5	Tell students it is time to review tootles from previous school day	N
6	Read a minimum of 3 tootles from previous school day	Y
7	Provide praise to the student- behavior was reported	N
8	Provide praise for the students that tootled	N
9	Count the total number of tootles reported on previous school day	Y
10	Update the Tootle Count	Y
11	Remind students of reward	N
12	If goal was met- 　－　when they will get their If goal not met- 　－　Let students know how many more tootles are needed to earn reward	N
		Total: 5/12 42%

As we can see from the data displayed above, Mr. Hogan is implementing the intervention with only 42% fidelity. While he is technically implementing tootling in the classroom, he is leaving out key components that will likely impact effectiveness. For example, he provides very little reinforcement to students for participation in the intervention or for exhibiting desired behaviors. Given that tootling is a reinforcement based intervention (this is what makes it effective) it is no wonder that students aren't engaging in the intervention or the target behaviors.

Dr. Evans met with Mr. Hogan after class to discuss the results. During the meeting, Mr. Hogan admitted that he really didn't think that the kids needed to be told that they were doing a good job, he felt they knew that he liked when they did what they were supposed to do. Dr. Evans stressed the importance of following all of the steps of the intervention, even if Mr. Hogan didn't think they were necessary. She asked him to give tootling one more week. During that week she asked if he would implement the intervention as it was written. If after that week it still wasn't working the team would develop a new intervention for his class. Dr. Evans visited the classroom 3 days that week and observed 100% fidelity during each visit.

At the end of the week Mr. Hogan met with the intervention team to determine if a new intervention was needed. At the meeting the teacher reported that the students had adapted well to the intervention and were suddenly "really in to it." Tootles had increased over the course of the week and the class had met the goal for reward one time and was likely to meet the goal again the next day. Mr. Hogan reported that the students were being much nicer to each other and that he would like to keep tootling in the classroom for a bit longer.

This example illustrates the effect that poor implementation fidelity can have on the outcomes of an intervention. In this case, Mr. Hogan believed it was the intervention that wasn't working. In fact, the intervention didn't have a chance to work, because it wasn't fully implemented. If the school psychologists had not collected fidelity data, the intervention would have likely been abandoned for something else. Whether or not a new intervention would be helpful is not known, but the time wasted on poorly implemented tootling along with the development, training, and implementation of a new intervention would be detrimental to the progress of the students in the classroom. Collecting data on the integrity of implementation prevented this waste of time and resources and ensured the success of tootling for this group of students. In the next chapter, we will discuss additional factors that may influence intervention effectiveness. The chapter will provide guidelines for how to troubleshoot when interventions are not having the expected results and methods for improving outcomes for students.

References

Anderson, M., & Daly, E. J. (2013). An experimental examination of the impact of choice of treatment components on treatment integrity. *Journal of Educational and Psychological Consultation*, 23(4), 231–263. https://doi.org/10.1080/10474412.2013.845493.

Borrelli, B. (2011). The assessment, monitoring, and enhancement of treatment fidelity in public health clinical trials. *Journal of Public Health Dentistry*, 71 Suppl 1, S52–S63.

Dane, A. V. and Schneider, B. H. (1998) Program integrity in primary and early secondary prevention: Are implementation effects out of control. *Clinical Psychology Review*, 18, 23–45. doi:10.1016/S0272-7358(97)00043-3.

Dunst, J., & Trivette, C.M. (1988). Helping, helplessness, and harm. In J. C. Witt, S. N. Elliott, & F. M. Gresham (Eds.) *Handbook of behavior therapy in education* (pp. 343–376). Plenum Press.

Durlak, J. A. and Dupre, E. P. (2008) Implementation Matters: A Review of Research on the Influence of Implementation on Program Outcomes and the Factors Affecting Implementation. *American Journal of Community Psychology*, 41, 327–350. http://dx.doi.org/10.1007/s10464-008-9165-0.

Gresham, F. M., Dart, E. H., & Collins, T. A. (2017). Generalizability of multiple measures of treatment integrity: Comparisons among direct observation, permanent products, and self-report. *School Psychology Review*, 46(1), 108–121. https://doi.org/10.17105/SPR46-1.108-121.

Gresham, F. M., MacMillan, D. L., Beebe-Frankenberger, M. E., & Bocian, K. M. (2000). Treatment integrity in learning disabilities intervention research: Do we really know how treatments are implemented? *Learning Disabilities Research and Practice*, 15(4), 198–205. https://doi.org/10.1207/SLDRP1504_4.

Noell G. H, Witt J. C, Slider N. J, Connell J. E, Gatti S. L, Williams K. L, et al. (2005). Treatment implementation following behavioral consultation in schools: A comparison of three follow-up strategies. *School Psychology Review*, 34, 87–106.

O'Donnell, C. L. (2008). Defining, conceptualizing, and measuring fidelity of implementation and its relationship to outcomes in K-12 curriculum intervention research. *Review of Educational Research*, 78(1), 33–84. https://doi.org/10.3102/0034654307313793.

Roach, A. T., Lawton, K., & Elliott, S. N. (2014). Bestpracticesinfacilitatingandevaluatingtheintegrityofschool–basedinterventions. *In Best Practices in School Psychology: Data-Based and Collaborative Decision Making* (pp. 133–146). NationalAssociation of School Psychologists

11 Troubleshooting Interventions

Identification of Modifications to Improve Outcomes

Alexandra Hilt-Panahon and Kennedi Alstead

Troubleshooting Interventions: Identification of Modifications to Improve Outcomes

When implementing an intervention, no matter how well planned or implemented, there are numerous things that can go wrong that may impact its effectiveness. Often, when this happens, professionals automatically jump to the conclusion that the intervention is not effective and that it should be abandoned for something new. When we do this, we may be "throwing the baby out with the bath water." Rather than jumping from one intervention to the next, it is best to evaluate the current intervention and determine if there is anything that can be changed or adapted to make the intervention more effective. This chapter will outline common problems encountered when implementing interventions in general and tootling specifically. While all possible potential problems cannot be covered here, we will outline the potential issues that could be affecting the overall outcomes of intervention.

Witt et al. (2004) outlined a four-step process for determining the impact of different variables on the effectiveness of behavioral interventions in schools. The authors noted the importance of the following four domains: (1) problem definition and monitoring, (2) fundamentals of classroom instruction and behavior management, (3) intervention integrity, and (4) intervention design. Each of these four domains play a vital role in the success of any intervention. We will look more closely at each and discuss ways to address concerns.

Defining the Problem

In order to determine the effectiveness of an intervention, in this case tootling, it is important to ensure that all individuals involved in the implementation of the intervention are clear about what the problem behavior is and how progress will be monitored. As discussed previously in Chapter 5 there needs to be an operational definition of the problem behavior that is observable and measurable. That definition must be used by all involved to evaluate changes in the frequency, duration, and/or intensity of the intervention. Changes are

DOI: 10.4324/9781003128663-14

determined through regular data collection and frequent progress monitoring. As we saw in the example of Ms. Bennett in Chapter 7, changing the operational definition may impact data and make it inaccurate. It is impossible to evaluate the change in behavior that can be attributed to the intervention if there are other factors influencing the data.

Classroom Instruction and Behavior Management

Chapter 4 of this book describes in detail the need for good instructional practices and strong classroom management skills in order to ensure the success of the tootling intervention. It is important, if an intervention is not working as expected, that an evaluation of the classroom environment and behavior management strategies is conducted. Often, many problems related to intervention effectiveness can be remedied with simple changes to overall classroom management. The following is a list of characteristics often found in classrooms. Every classroom has some of these things in place, no classroom has them all. Please review the list and decide which items are present in your classroom and which are not. While you may have done some of these things in the past, think carefully about your current classroom and what is happening right now.

As stated above, no classroom will have all of these things in place. The more that are present, however, the more likely the classroom runs smoothly and students learn. Classrooms with a large percentage of these variables in place are more likely to have students who are successful both academically and behaviorally (Sprick et al., 2021).

Classroom Structure

Classroom structure refers to the mechanisms in place that maintain order and organization in the setting. Establishing a clear structure for the classroom allows students the opportunity to learn and engage in a positive way. Classroom structure takes into account the schedules, activities, transitions, and rules in place in the setting and how they are taught and reinforced.

A classroom with a strong structure has set schedules that are followed throughout the day. Students and teachers know the schedule and follow it consistently. Providing students with a predictable schedule allows them to know what will be happening to them and when. This can alleviate anxiety and reduce problem behaviors that are caused by uncertainty (Scott et al., 2007)

Schedules should be posted in the room and written in a way that all students can understand. The schedule is reviewed frequently and is consistently followed. In addition, all students know what the schedule is and are able to follow it.

Materials and Activities

In order to maintain a positive learning environment within the classroom, proper preparation of the materials and activities that will be used in the classroom should be a priority. The activities that will occur throughout the day must be planned and prepped prior to the start of the day. While this is difficult for teachers and other professionals given the demands on time, it is imperative for student success and will provide for better student outcomes. In addition to good planning, execution of those plans is also important to success. Well-structured classrooms are able to follow the schedule and complete all planned activities within the time allotted.

Transitions are a time in school settings that can be problematic for students and adults alike. It is important to ensure that there is structure and procedures around these times as well as during the more instructional academic learning times. This includes providing students warnings prior to transitions and ensuring procedures are in place to allow for smooth transitions with little problem behavior.

As discussed in detail in Chapter 4, rules and expectations are necessary for a well-structured classroom. Rules give students the structure needed to be successful both academically and socially. All rules should be developed prior to students entering the classroom or at the beginning of the school year with student input. Rules should be posted and all students should know the rules of the classroom. For more information related to the development and implementation of classroom rules and expectations, see Chapter 4.

Academic Instruction

Another factor in a successful classroom is the quality and quantity of instruction provided to students. Evaluating the quality of instruction is as important in making sure that it occurs. Some things to consider when evaluating the effectiveness of instruction in the classroom are described below.

Student success and continued progress should be first and foremost in the setting. In order to ensure this, several actions on the part of the teacher or other professionals should be taken. These include having strategies in place for regularly monitoring student progress to ensure that everyone is making adequate progress toward goals. In the classroom, teachers should know the instructional levels of all students in the classroom and instruction should be tailored to that level to the extent possible. Whether in a classroom or some other setting, there should be frequent checks for understanding to determine if children and learning what they need to learn. Along with this, children should have multiple opportunities to ask and answer questions to further ensure understanding.

When designing both group and individual activities it is important to keep in mind the length of the activity and the students' ability to attend. If asking children to complete work independently, be sure that they are able to complete that work with a high level of accuracy. Finally, it is important to create an environment in which all expectations are clear and where children are engaged.

Treatment Integrity

Treatment integrity is vital to the success of any intervention, and tootling is no exception. This aspect of intervention implementation is so important to the effectiveness of an intervention we have devoted an entire chapter of this book to the research demonstrating the importance of ensuring integrity in the implementation of classroom-based interventions. Provided here is a brief summary of the treatment integrity research and discussion of its importance to the effectiveness of an intervention. A more detailed review of the topic can be found in Chapter 9.

Treatment integrity is defined as implementing an intervention in the manner in which it was intended (Sanetti & Kratchowill, 2009). Research has shown that implementing interventions with integrity increases the likelihood of their success (Gresham, 1989). Despite the importance of treatment integrity (also referred to as treatment fidelity), we know that teachers typically do not maintain integrity of implementation much longer than a week (Gresham et al., 2000). Once integrity declines, the effectiveness of the intervention does as well. This often leads teachers to believe that the intervention doesn't work, when it is instead the fact that the intervention wasn't implemented as intended.

Intervention Design

If after evaluating all other variables in the setting you find that it is generally well managed, structured, and organized both academically and behaviorally and the intervention is properly executed you must then question whether or not the intervention itself is the problem (Witt et al., 2004). There are several reasons why the intervention may not be appropriate. First, you should make sure that the intervention is designed to address the problem. If an intervention is being used to target a behavior for which it was not designed, there is little likelihood of success. For example, a surgeon may perform a heart transplant to perfection, but if the patient's liver is failing the heart surgery won't solve the problem. Often, interventions are chosen based on the interventionist's knowledge of that intervention, success with it in the past, or the recommendation of a colleague. While these are important, if it is not matched to the student's needs it will not be successful.

Other Considerations

In addition to the considerations listed above, there are other practical aspects of the intervention to consider if things are not progressing as predicted. First, you should consider if the intervention you have developed is fully in alignment with the culture of the setting you are implementing it in. Do you have buy-in from all of the stakeholders involved? Whatever intervention program you plan to use, it should be something that everyone involved believes in and will participate in fully. If there are aspects of the program that people don't agree with or goes against their beliefs, it will be less likely that they will implement it with integrity. For example, if one of the paraprofessionals working with a student doesn't think that giving children rewards is a good idea, they may be less likely to encourage students to participate in tootling. While this isn't necessarily a direct breach of implementation fidelity, it could certainly impact children's morale around the intervention. If staff are not enthusiastic about an intervention program, it is less likely that children will be as well.

You also need to consider how the tootling intervention will fit with other programs and interventions that are already in place for individual children and the group as a whole. Before implementing any new program, you should be sure that it will add value, rather than distract from what is already in place. Teachers and other school personnel are constantly having new initiatives introduced, often without their input or buy-in. Often, many of these initiatives conflict with one another and create additional or redundant work for school professionals. This leads to low morale, low fidelity, and low levels of effectiveness. Adding something new will be less likely to be effective in situations like this. To this end, it is vital that all intervention programing take into account all aspects of the environment in which the intervention will be implemented. Consider the following questions to determine if implementation is appropriate.

1   What other interventions, initiatives, programming is in place currently?
2   Will the (tootling) intervention interfere with any of the current programs in place?
3   Does the staff that will be implementing the (tootling) intervention have the ability to implement with integrity given the current demands on time and resources?
4   Is the intervention overly complicated or involved?

If the answer to these questions indicate that it will be difficult for staff you should consider what changes can be made to make implementation more feasible. First, consider what is in place that is mandatory and cannot be changed. This could be initiatives from administration or other interventions that have been shown to be effective for individuals or the group as a whole. Next, look at things that are not necessary and evaluate if continuation of them is warranted. There is no reason to continue with a program if it is ineffective or no longer necessary. Finally, look to see if there is a way to incorporate tootling into the existing structure in a way that will be simple for all stakeholders. If you cannot do this, then it is best not to introduce it until you can.

By evaluating the intervention as described in this chapter, you will be able to determine if tootling is the right intervention, if it is being implemented correctly by all professionals, and what adjustments need to be made to most effectively address the social skills of children in your classroom or therapeutic setting. This step in intervention implementation is vital to successful educational interventions because it provides a mechanism to ensure successful outcomes without wasting time, energy, and resources on unnecessary intervention changes. It also allows the interventionist to know when, in fact, an intervention is not working and will not end in positive outcomes for the student or students in question. This allows educators to make educated, data-based decisions about which interventions to use and when changes are necessary.

References

Gresham, F. M. (1989). Assessment of treatment integrity in school consultation and prereferral intervention. *School Psychology Review*, 18(1), 37–50. https://doi.org/10.1080/02796015.1989.12085399.

Gresham, F. M., MacMillan, D. L., Beebe-Frankenberger, M. E., & Bocian, K. M. (2000). Treatment integrity in learning disabilities intervention research: Do we really know how treatments are implemented? *Learning Disabilities Research and Practice*, 15(4), 198–205. https://doi.org/10.1207/SLDRP1504_4.

Sanetti, L. M. H., & Kratchowill, T. R. (2009). Toward developing a science of treatment integrity: Introduction to the special series. *School Psychology Review*, 38(4), 445–459.

Scott, T. M., Park, K. L., Swain-Bradway, J., & Landers, E. (2007). Positive behavior support in the classroom: Facilitating behaviorally inclusive learning environments. *International Journal of Behavioral and Consultation Therapy*, 3(2), 223–235. https://doi.org/10.1037/h0100800.

Sprick, J., Sprick, R., Edwards, J., & Coughlin, C. (2021). *CHAMPS: A proactive & positive approach to classroom management*. (3rd ed.). Ancora. https://ancorapublishing.com/product/champs-third-edition/.

Witt, J. C., VanDerHeyden, A. M., & Gilbertson, D. (2004). Troubleshooting behavioral interventions: A systematic process for finding and eliminating problems. *School Psychology Review*, 33(3), 363–383. https://doi.org/10.1080/02796015.2004.12086254.

12 Tootling Case Studies

Alexandra Hilt-Panahon and Kennedi Alstead

Tootling Case Studies

In this final chapter, a few case study examples will be described in order to provide a deeper understanding of how to implement tootling within a variety of settings. First, we provide an example of an empirical evaluation of the tootling intervention in a general education setting. Second, we provide an additional example of an empirical evaluation of the tootling intervention in a special education setting, specifically an Emotional/Behavioral Disorders (EBD) classroom. Third, we describe an implementation that was led by school staff, and lastly, we address the use of tootling in a non-academic setting. Each example provides descriptions of how the tootling intervention can be implemented in a variety of settings with different children and adolescents. These case studies are fictional, but based on students and classrooms with whom the authors of this book have worked.

Case Study #1: Tootling in a General Education Classroom with a Student with Autism Spectrum Disorder

Oliver Wilson, a ten-year-old boy diagnosed with Autism Spectrum Disorder, was a new student in Ms. Wall's general education fourth grade classroom. Oliver had moved to the area after his father was relocated for work. Ms. Wall wanted to help Oliver adapt to his new classroom and thought that meeting with his family would help her to know how best to do that. Ms. Wall set up a meeting with the family shortly after he started in her classroom.

The meeting was held after school in Ms. Wall's classroom. Ms. Wilson arrived to the meeting on time, with her three younger children with her. Oliver greeted his siblings after prompting from his mother. He said hello to Joey (five), Marissa (four) and Jolene (two). Ms. Wilson apologized for bringing the other children with her, but said that she did not have child care so she had to bring them. Ms. Wall gave the children some crayons and paper to draw while she and Ms. Wilson talked.

Ms. Wall thanked Oliver's mother for meeting with her and let her know that she wanted learn more about Oliver in order to determine the best ways

DOI: 10.4324/9781003128663-15

to help him be successful at his new school. She asked Ms. Wilson to tell her about Oliver's strengths. Ms. Wilson said that Oliver was smart and did well in school if he has the right supports. He likes being around adults, more so than peers. When asked about his challenges, Oliver's mother told Ms. Wall that she was concerned that it was hard for him to make friends. She said that he doesn't really interact much with his siblings or the other kids in their old neighborhood. She said that he never had playdates at his old school, and was usually not invited to birthday parties or sleepovers. Ms. Wilson stated that Oliver's behavior therapist was working on increasing social skills before they moved, but that he had not had much opportunity to practice those skills before they relocated.

After talking with Oliver's mom, Ms. Wall decided that implementing an intervention that allowed Oliver to practice his social skills would be beneficial for Oliver and hopefully help him to make new friends. After talking with the social worker and doing some research, she decided that Tootling would be a great option for her classroom. She had seen this intervention used in a classroom during her student teaching a few years ago, and knew that students responded well to the intervention. She decided to solicit the help of the building school psychologist, Dr. Reese, with implementation. Dr. Reese was excited for the opportunity. After the intervention was complete, she suggested to Ms. Wall that they write a paper that described what they did and publish it so other teachers and school personnel could use the intervention as well. The following section includes the method, results, and discussion from the paper.

This study was conducted with a target student in mind who was diagnosed with autism spectrum disorder (ASD) and was receiving special education services under the special education category of ASD. The intervention was still implemented with the whole class; however, the authors wanted to determine if tootling was effective in increasing academic engagement and decreasing disruptive behavior for a student with ASD through the implementation of a class-wide intervention. In doing this, the authors would be able to suggest the use of tootling in the majority of inclusive general education classrooms if tootling showed to increase positive behavioral change for this student. Throughout the case study, references to previous chapters will be made, so the reader can reference those previous chapters for more information.

Prior to the start of the study, one of the authors met with the principal and a special education teacher at an intermediate school in the Midwest. The study was described to both the principal and special education teacher, and a request for potential participants was made. The special education teacher identified the target student with ASD, discussed with the general education teacher who had that student in their classroom, and sent the informed consent form to the student's family prior to the authors meeting the student. A consent form was sent home to the parents due to the authors being visitors to the school that were going to collect individual data on their child with possible intentions of sharing this information with other individuals. Without consent provided by the parents, the authors would not be able to conduct observations on the student. If the intervention is being conducted by the classroom teacher only for his/her own classroom management, this step may not be as important. However, it would still be important for the teacher to mention this activity that will be implemented in the classroom to parents to allow for transparency and increase family and school collaboration. For this specific case study, once consent was obtained, the authors met with the general education teacher to explain the intervention in greater detail and answer any questions the teacher had.

Participants in this case study included the general education classroom teacher, a 4th-grade classroom in an intermediate school in the Midwest, and a target student with ASD, named Oliver. The teacher reported his common problem behaviors were talking out of turn, being out-of-seat when it is expected to be in his seat, pounding on his desk, and shouting. The importance of determining problem behaviors ahead of time is to help to determine the effectiveness of the intervention on creating behavioral change. For example, the authors used this information to guide their observations and determine if tootling decreased these reported problem behaviors.

Observations were conducted in the classroom by the authors during whole group math instruction during the first period of the day, starting at 8:20am and ending at 8:30am. Typical instruction consisted of a whole group math lesson, individual work time, and then whole group opportunities to respond. However, tootling was implemented throughout the entire school day, but the authors were just able to observe during the 10-minute time period. Again, if tootling is implemented by the classroom teacher, the teacher can decide which 10–15-minute time period they would like to select for observation of behavior or data collection. It may be best to observe behavior during a less structured time, such as group work or break time to allow for more opportunities for prosocial behavior.

Materials Used

Materials that were used for this specific study will be listed below. Many of these materials were mentioned in Chapter 6; however, through this case study, the reader will be able to identify how to incorporate the materials to meet specific needs of the classroom.

Tootle Cards

Students used pre-made tootle cards to record observations of their peers' prosocial behaviors within the special education classrooms. Tootle cards typically have space for students to write their tootle without any prompts. For this study, each card took up one-third of a sheet of 8 x11 paper. Each tootle card consisted of places for the student to write their peer's name who engaged in the prosocial behavior, what prosocial behavior their peer engaged in, and their own name (the tootler). The tootling cards were the same as demonstrated within Chapter 6: How to Implement Tootling. When students wanted to write a tootle, they walked over to the tootle box, wrote a tootle card, and put the tootle card in the tootle box. Students were asked to wait until large group instruction was over to write a tootle.

Tootle Box

After recording a tootle, students placed the tootle cards in a large, clear container labeled *Tootles* that was kept near the classroom door in an easily accessible area of the classroom. Using a clear container enables the students to have a visual representation of their progress towards their class goal. Common containers used are plastic cereal containers or large plastic jars.

Tootle Thermometer

A dry erase poster with an image of a thermometer was displayed in the front of the classroom during the tootling phases to provide feedback to the students regarding the daily number of tootles their peers reported. The goal was displayed at the top of the thermometer and their progress was recorded every morning. This also served as a reminder of the number of tootles required to reach the class goal. Again, depending on the needs of the classroom, this visual representation of progress toward the goal can be done in a variety of ways without the need to purchase a dry-erase thermometer. Tallies can be written on a white board at the end of each class period to depict the current number of tootles collected, or an updated number of current tootles out of their class goal can be updated every day as well.

Rewards

Class-wide rewards were selected by the students with the teacher and authors present to regulate the selection. After discussing the options, students were asked to vote on their most preferred reward. The reward with the majority of the votes was then be selected. By having the students generate their own reward preferences, the reward is then more reinforcing than if the teacher or author chose the reward for them. Common reward choices are pizza parties, dessert parties or extra recess time. As mentioned in Chapter 8: Modifications for Grade Levels, reward choices may differ depending on the age of the students participating in the intervention. The entire class earned the reward that received the majority of votes upon reaching their collective tootle goal. After the reward was earned, new ideas were generated by the students and a new vote was taken.

Data Collection Sheet

Throughout baseline and intervention phases, a data collection form created by the authors was used for the study. This form included the operational definitions of each dependent variable observed, as well as numbered intervals with boxes labeled for each behavior for observers to record during each 10-second interval. Every fifth interval was marked as a peer comparison. During this interval, instead of reporting on Oliver's on-task, disruptive and prosocial behavior, a same-age, same-sex peer was observed. The peers were selected based on a round robin approach in the classroom. A free interval timer application (i.e., Simple Repeat Timer) on a smart phone and headphones were also used. This app makes a sound indicating the beginning of each new interval.

Even if the implementation of tooling is not used for research purposes, it is always helpful to record the effectiveness of the intervention on the class's behavior to determine effectiveness of the intervention. An option for teachers to record observed behavior could be selecting a specific time period a few days per week to tally the amount of observed prosocial behavior or disruptive behavior during that set time period. Then, the teacher could keep track of progress on some sort of running document. In order to determine effectiveness, the teacher would hope to see a decrease in disruptive behavior and an increase in prosocial behavior.

How to Determine Behavior Change

In order to determine the effectiveness of tooling on both the target student's behavior and the entire class's behavior, specific behaviors were observed and measured. Oliver's on-task behavior was the primary behavior examined in this study. Typically, this is done for the whole class. On-task behavior was defined as the student being engaged (e.g., passively or actively) in an assigned activity. Examples included the student sitting in their seat, following along in a book, answering teacher-asked questions, sitting quietly while the teacher is talking, working independently at their desk, and raising their hand to ask a question. Non-examples included playing with items not related to the task, talking to peers when the student was expected to be attending to the teacher or task, and putting their head on the desk. On-task behavior was measured using 10-second momentary time sampling procedures. Therefore, the authors indicated Oliver (and his peer comparison) being on-task or off-task at the beginning of the 10-second interval. Peer comparison data was collected every fifth interval using same-age, same-sex peers using a round robin approach.

Disruptive behavior was one of the other behaviors that was observed and was recorded when Oliver engaged in any behavior that was distracting to the class. A partial-interval recording system was used to measure disruptive behavior, meaning that Oliver (or his peer comparison) was observed throughout the entire 10-second interval if they engaged in any disruptive behavior. Examples included talking out of turn, pounding on desk, and walking around classroom when it was expected to be seated. Non-examples included inaudibly asking a peer for assistance on a task, doodling, day-dreaming, looking out the window or around the room. Peer comparison data was collected every fifth interval using same-age, same-sex peers in the classroom.

Prosocial behavior was the final behavior that was observed and was recorded using partial-interval procedures (similar process as disruptive behavior). Prosocial behavior was recorded when Oliver had a positive social interaction with another student. Examples included helping a student with their homework, answering a peer's question, giving another student a compliment, playing with a peer, and working on an assignment together when it was allowed. Non-examples included answering a teacher's question, obeying classroom rules, and giving a teacher a compliment. Peer comparison data was collected every fifth interval using same-age, same-sex peers using a round robin approach.

As previously mentioned, the author's sole purpose in the classroom was to observe the behavior of the students. If the classroom teacher is the one implementing the intervention, it may not be feasible to keep track of on-task behavior the specific way that was mentioned. Or, the classroom teacher may only be able to keep track of on-task behavior for 5-minutes per observation period instead of 10–15 minutes. Any method of data collection that is feasible for the teacher to use to keep track of behavior change, is recommended by the authors. Additionally, tallies for disruptive and prosocial behavior during that 5-minute time period can also supplement the on-task behavior data for observed behavior change.

Observation Sessions, Training, Implementation

Observations occurred in the classroom for 10 minutes, three to four days per week. Observation data was collected on Oliver, including peer comparisons every fifth interval. Oliver's behavior was observed for four intervals, then a round robin approach was used to determine which peer would be observed during the fifth interval. These students were selected before the observation period and were same-age, same-sex peers. Each peer comparison was assigned a number prior to the start of the observation. Peers were then observed in that order throughout the observation, regardless of their position in the room. Observers began observing Oliver at the beginning of the 10-second interval and recorded whether the student was on-task. During the remaining part of each interval, observers recorded if Oliver engaged in disruptive or prosocial behavior. Upon hearing the interval cue, the observer moved onto the next interval and repeated the steps three more times. Once it became the fifth interval, the authors observed the first peer comparison the same way as Oliver. This process repeated until all intervals in the 10-minute observation period were completed. Four peer comparisons were used during each observation period.

Training the interventionist in the intervention is one of the most important factors for successful implementation, which is one of the purposes of this text. Within this study, the teacher was trained in the use of the tootling intervention by the first author during one session prior to the start of data collection. The author described what tootling was and how it is typically implemented. Then, protocols for student training and intervention sessions were shared with the teacher, and all questions were answered prior to implementation of tootling. Ensuring that the interventionist understands all aspects of the intervention before implementation is extremely important. The interventionist could practice a typical day of implementation before officially implementing it in the classroom.

Before implementing tootling in the classroom, the authors sought to observe the class and the target student to determine the current levels of on-task behavior, disruptive behavior, and prosocial behavior. Observations before implementation of tootling are relevant to ensure that tootling was the main cause of behavior change.

Prior to the implementation of tootling procedures, one 20-minute training session was conducted with the students. As mentioned in Chapter 6, the students can be trained either in one or two training sessions, depending on how well the students are responding to the initial training session. The training session was completed by the first author with help from the classroom teacher. During this training session, the author explained what tootling was and why it was important to implement in a classroom setting. The author provided and examples and non-examples of prosocial behaviors to the students to help them understand what they would be reporting of their peers. The author and the teacher engaged in a role play activity where the teacher engaged in a prosocial behavior (i.e., helping the author with a question she had). The students were then provided with the opportunity to raise their hand and orally describe examples of prosocial behaviors. The author provided feedback and praise to the student on their example. Afterwards, the author described how to write a tootle and where to find the tootle cards. The purpose of the tootle box was explained, as well as the goal thermometer.

Another helpful tip for training students in the tootling intervention, would be to allow time for them to practice writing a tootle. This way, the interventionist can visually determine how well the students are responding to the training session or if additional training sessions are needed to practice writing tootles. Feedback and praise from the interventionist can be provided during this time as well.

During tootling sessions, tootle cards were placed by the tootle box, which was located by the classroom door. Students were prompted at the beginning of each period by the classroom teacher to write tootles if they observed their peer engaging in prosocial behaviors. Throughout the day, students were able to write tootles for their peers. This was encouraged during passing periods or free time to not interrupt instruction. Students were reminded to submit completed tootles to the classroom tootling box. A class-wide reward was also used in combination with the tootling intervention. Specifically, the teacher and author collaborated to set an appropriate goal for a number of tootles to be reached by the class in order to earn a group reward. Students were then asked to identify a reward when the goal was researched. Students provided ideas for rewards and then the class voted to determine which item would serve as the reward. After a reward was earned, this process was repeated and a new reward was chosen. Examples of rewards included additional recess time, a cookie party, or a pizza party.

At the beginning of each day, the teacher read the completed tootles from the previous day aloud and counted the number of appropriately reported tootles towards the class goal. The number of tootles produced that day were added to the feedback chart (i.e., dry erase thermometer) so students could see their progress towards their cumulative goal. If the students reached their goal, they earned their reward the next day.

Results

In this section, the authors will describe the overall results of the case study. Specifically, how did tootling impact on-task behavior, disruptive behavior, and prosocial behavior for Oliver, as well as his peers? Table 12.1 shows the percentage of intervals observed with on-task behavior, disruptive behavior, and prosocial behavior from the student with ASD during baseline and intervention phases when tootling was implemented in the entire classroom. When tootling was not implementing initially, there were zero instances of prosocial behavior, Oliver was on-task 69.8% of observation periods and engaged in disruptive behavior 12% of intervals. There were varying levels of on-task behavior; however, the baseline phase ended in a decreasing trend. Peer on-task behavior was higher, with a median score of 79% of observed intervals.

Once tootling was implemented, there was one instance of prosocial behavior observed (1%), Oliver was observed to be on-task 89.5% of intervals, with an increasing trend, and his disruptive behavior decreased to 2.5%. During the first tootling phase, peers were on-task 83% of intervals. When tootling was removed from the classroom, there were again zero instances of prosocial behavior observed, his on-task behavior decreased to 46.7% (peer median on-task =83%) and he engaged in disruptive behavior 19.3% of the time during the observation periods. An increasing trend was observed for on-task behavior and decreasing trend was observed for disruptive behavior; however, the level of the two is a vast difference compared to the intervention phases. Tootling was reimplemented in the classroom for the final time, Oliver did not engage in any prosocial behaviors during the observation periods, was observed to be on-task 96.7% of intervals

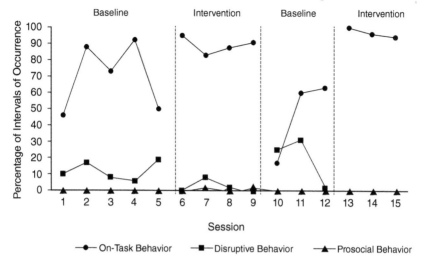

Figure 12.1 Effects of Tootling on Behavior for a Student with ASD in a General Education Classroom

(peer=100%) and engaged in little disruptive behaviors (0.7%). Figure 12.1 also depicts the impact of tootling on Oliver's on-task behavior, disruptive behavior, and prosocial behavior.

The results of this study indicate that Tootling is an effective intervention for a student with ASD educated in a general education classroom. Results showed that the student's on-task behavior increased, while disruptive behavior decreased. Prosocial behavior increased slightly when tootling was implemented. In addition to positive outcomes for the target student, mean on-task behaviors for general education students increased during intervention as well. While baseline levels of on-task for these students was already at acceptable levels (~ 80%), increased engagement is always a desired outcome. On-task behavior increased for those students in general education who took part in the tootling intervention. In fact, on-task behavior increased by 10% of intervals during tootling, reaching close to 100% during the second administration.

Table 12.1 Average Percentage of Intervals with On-Task, Prosocial, and Disruptive Behavior

	On-Task Behavior	Disruptive Behavior	Prosocial Behavior
Baseline	69.8%	12%	0%
Tootling	89.5%	2.5%	1%
Baseline	46.7%	19.3%	0%
Tootling	96.7%	0.7%	0%

Case Study #2: Tootling for Students with Emotional/Behavioral Disorders

The purpose of this study was to determine the effectiveness of tootling within an Emotional/Behavioral Disorders (EBD) classroom. Participants in this study included one teacher and three students in a school-based therapeutic academic program in an intermediate school in the Midwest. The school has approximately 425 students enrolled with 81% of students identified as white, 9% Hispanic, 5% two or more races, 4% African American, and 1% Asian. Thirty eight percent of students at the school received free/reduced lunch. The program provides access to integrated special education planning along with therapeutic support for students. Therapeutic supports included social skills training, counseling, and a variety of behavioral and cognitive behavioral interventions. There were also two paraprofessionals who worked with students in the classroom. The paraprofessionals were not directly involved in the implementation of the tootling intervention, but they did provide assistance to students who needed help filling out tootle cards.

The participating classroom was selected by asking the special education teacher if she would like her class to participate in the intervention. The teacher was licensed in both general and special education and had taught in this program for the last seven years. Parental consent from the parents and guardians of all three students in the class was obtained. Therefore, all students in the classroom participated in the intervention. There were three students in the classroom during the period when data were collected. All three students were male. One student was in second grade, one in fifth, and one in sixth. The students spent the majority of the day in the therapeutic classroom, with time in the general education classroom to the extent possible. Participants had been in this setting for varied amounts of time (one month to four years) depending on the students' needs. In addition to an educational label of EBD, students also had a variety of medical diagnoses including Attention-Deficit/Hyperactivity Disorder (ADHD) and Oppositional Defiant Disorder (ODD). It should be noted that these students were at times absent from school or removed from the classroom given the severity of student behaviors.

Materials Used

Most of the materials listed below are very similar to the materials referenced within Case Study #1. However, many of the materials needed to be modified due to the nature of the EBD classroom within this study. It is important to note the differences between the two and to continue to determine possible necessary modifications for tootling within different settings.

Tootle Cards

Students used pre-made tootle cards to record observations of their peers' pro-social behaviors within the special education classrooms. The tootle cards were modified for the purpose of this study to make them easier for students in the special education classroom to use. Typical tootle cards have space for students to write their tootle without any prompts. For this study, each card took up half of a sheet of 8 x11 paper and had a box for students to check "who," "did what," and "for who." All students' names were listed under the "who" and "for who" with check boxes next to each name. Examples of prosocial behaviors (i.e., answered a peer's question, shared, helped) were listed under the "did what" column, as well as a blank line for students to write in their own observed prosocial behaviors. This column also had check boxes next to each behavior so students did not have to write a full sentence on their own if they could not or did not want to write.

Tootle Box and Tootle Thermometer

The tootle box was a large, clear container labeled *Tootles* that was kept near the teacher's desk. This easily accessible area of the classroom was chosen so students could place their tootle cards in after recording a tootle. A dry erase poster with an image of a thermometer was displayed in the front of the classroom during the tootling phases to provide feedback to the students regarding the daily number of tootles reported by the class. This also served as a reminder of the number of tootles required to reach the class goal.

Rewards

Rewards were selected by the students from a list approved by the teacher. The approved list included rewards such as a pizza and donut party. Students were provided a choice to determine what would be most reinforcing. Students voted on the choices and the entire class earned the reward that received the majority of votes upon reaching their collective goal of predetermined tootles. After the reward was earned, a new list was generated, and a new vote was taken at the beginning of the next session.

Data Collection Sheet

Throughout baseline and intervention phases, a data collection form created by the researchers was used for the study. This form included the operational definitions of each dependent variable observed, as well as numbered intervals with boxes labeled for each behavior for observers to record during each 10-second interval. A free interval timer application (i.e., Simple Repeat Timer) on a smart phone and headphones were also used. This app makes a sound indicating the beginning of each new interval.

Tootling Log

The teacher kept track of the total number of appropriate tootles produced each day in the tootling log. There were directions on the top of the log that asked the teacher to record the number of tootles the class submitted each day after the tootles were reviewed. There was also a checkbox next to the class goal to indicate whether the goal was reached that day

How to Determine Behavior Change

Students' on-task behavior was the primary behavior examined in this study and was used to decide when to add and remove the tootling intervention in the classroom. While disruptive and pro-social behaviors were of interest to both the researchers and classroom teacher, on-task was chosen as the primary behavior because observations were conducted during academic periods when on-task behavior would be the primary expectation. In addition, students who are on-task are less likely to be disruptive, making on-task ideal for decision making purposes. On-task behavior was defined as a student being engaged (e.g., passively or actively) in an assigned activity. Examples included a student sitting in their seat, following along in a book, answering teacher-asked questions, sitting quietly while the teacher is talking, working independently at their desk, and raising their hand to ask a question. Non-examples included playing with items not related to the task, talking to peers when the student was expected to be attending to the teacher or task, and putting their head on the desk.

Disruptive Behavior

Disruptive behavior was a secondary behavior observed and was recorded when a student engaged in any behavior that was distracting to the class. Examples included yelling, cursing, throwing objects, non-compliance, and aggression. Non-examples included inaudibly asking a peer for assistance on a task, doodling, daydreaming, and looking out the window or around the room.

Prosocial Behavior

Prosocial behavior was another secondary behavior. Prosocial behavior was recorded when the target student had a positive social interaction with another student. Prosocial behaviors was also indirectly measured by each teacher through a daily count of the number of tootles that meet criteria (i.e., tootles that appropriately indicate "who," "did what," "for whom"). Examples included helping a student with their homework, answering a peer's question, giving another student a compliment, playing with a peer, and working on an assignment together when it was allowed. Non-examples included answering a teacher's question, obeying classroom rules, and giving a teacher a compliment.

Observation Sessions

Data were collected during 15-minute observation sessions. Observers collected data from an unobtrusive location in the classroom to avoid distracting students.

A 10-second momentary time sampling recording procedure was used to measure students' on-task behavior. When using momentary time sampling, a behavior is scored as either present or absent during the moment that a timed interval began. Throughout the remaining seconds of the interval, that behavior is not evaluated. Momentary time sampling provides the least biased estimate of behavior.

Disruptive and prosocial behaviors were measured using partial interval recording. Partial interval recording is a form of interval recording in which the behavior is scored as having occurred if at least one instance of the target behavior is observed during any part of the interval. Partial interval recording is useful when observing behaviors that occur at relatively low rates or behaviors that are somewhat inconsistent in duration, thus making it a useful method for measuring disruptive and prosocial behaviors. During data collection, an interval timer application was used on researchers' phones with a set of headphones to notify observers of the start of each interval.

Observations occurred at the same time each day in a round robin style in the classroom for 15 minutes, two to four days per week. Each student in the class was assigned a number prior to the start of the observation. Students were then observed in that order throughout the observation, regardless of their position in the room. Observers began observing student #1 at the beginning of the 10-second interval and recorded whether the student was on-task. During the remaining part of each interval, observers recorded if the target student engaged in disruptive or prosocial behavior. Upon hearing the interval cue, the observer moved to student #2 in the predetermined order. Once all students in the classroom were observed, the rotation restarted until all intervals in the 15-minute observation period were completed. Data were reported as the class-wide percentage of intervals of occurrence for each dependent variable. This percentage was calculated by dividing the total number of intervals of occurrence by the total number of intervals in the observation, and then multiplying the result by 100.

Training and Implementation

The teacher was trained in the use of the tootling intervention during one 30-minute session prior to the start of data collection. The researcher described what tootling was and how it is implemented. The protocols for student training and intervention sessions were shared with the teacher. The teacher was given a script to help guide her through the training session. The researcher and teacher role played the implementation of training the students and implementing tootling. Role play consisted of the researcher playing the role of the teacher and demonstrating how to implement training. After answering the teacher's questions, the roles were then reversed, and the teacher practiced the implementation of training with the researcher playing the role of student. The same procedures were followed when role playing intervention implementation.

Prior to Tootling Implementation

Baseline sessions occurred during math class. During these sessions, the classroom teacher conducted business as usual. Observations were conducted during a group math lesson scheduled in the morning. Students sat at their desks facing the Smartboard. The teacher stood in front of the class and taught lessons at the Smartboard. Paraprofessionals remained at the back of the classroom during group instruction and then sat with individual students who needed assistance with independent group work. During this time, researchers sat on one side of the classroom where both the teacher and the students could be easily observed. Researchers observed students' on-task, disruptive, and prosocial behaviors in the manner described above.

Student Training

Prior to the implementation of tootling procedures, two 20-minute training sessions were conducted with the students over two days. The training sessions were co-facilitated by the classroom teacher and the first author. Before reading the script to students, the primary investigator read through the script with the teacher to ensure understanding of each step. During the first day of training, students were provided with examples and non-examples of classmates' helping behaviors. Students were asked to give their own examples of how they help others at home and at school. Tattling and tootling were defined, and students were given examples of tootling (e.g., helping a student pick up their books, loaning a student a pencil, showing a student how to work through a math problem). Students then verbally provided their own examples. Responses that fit criteria (i.e., who/classmate did what/helpful behavior, and for whom/who they helped) for tootling were praised, and corrective feedback was provided when students gave examples that did not fit the criteria. Corrective feedback was verbally provided by the first author and teacher. Students were told why their example did not fit the criteria and an appropriate alternative was then written. The students were taught the tootling procedures. Students were asked to either write their own examples of tootles or to use the pre-made checkbox tootle cards (described in the following paragraph). Examples were collected and shared with the class. The purpose of the tootling box was explained, as well as the goal thermometer. Examples were read aloud, and praise and corrective feedback were given by the teacher to students.

On the second day of student training, the definition for tootling was reviewed and students were reminded that tootling involves only their classmates' prosocial behaviors. Tootling procedures were reviewed and students practiced writing their own examples of tootles on index cards. Students were given the option to use "check box" cards instead of creating their own tootles, with the intent of increasing compliance and encouraging students to tootle. The pre-made cards gave students the option of checking their classmate's name on the tootle rather than writing it out on their own. Examples were collected and shared with the class. The purpose of the tootling box and the goal thermometer were revisited.

Tootling

For tootling sessions, the lessons were conducted by the teacher in the same manner as described in the baseline condition. In addition to typical classroom instruction, the tootling intervention was implemented. The classroom teacher provided students with tootle cards to keep at their desks, so they were able to record instances of prosocial peer behaviors throughout the time they were in the classroom. Tootling instructions were briefly reviewed by the teachers and the students were encouraged to write a tootle if they observed a classmate engaging in prosocial behavior. Students were reminded to submit completed tootles to the classroom tootling box. An interdependent group contingency procedure was implemented in combination with the tootling intervention. Specifically, the teacher and researcher collaborated to set an appropriate goal for a number of tootles to be reached by the class to earn a group reward. Students were then asked to identify a reward they would like to earn when the goal was reached. Students provided ideas for rewards and then the class voted to determine which item would serve as the reward. After a reward was earned, this process was repeated, and a new reward was chosen. Examples of rewards included additional recess time, a cookie party, or a pizza party.

At the beginning of each day, the teacher read the completed tootles from the previous day aloud and counted the number of appropriately reported tootles towards the class goal. The number of tootles produced that day were added to the feedback chart (i.e., dry erase thermometer) so students could see their progress towards their cumulative goal. At the end of the day, the teacher completed the tootle log, which consisted of entering the number of tootles written that day as well as if the students had reached the tootle goal. If the students reached their goal, the teacher notified the first author who brought the reward the next morning. The students would receive the reward during the morning tootle time, after the teacher read the tootles and marked progress on the goal thermometer. A tootling checklist comprised of five items (e.g., "previous day's tootles are read aloud," "blank tootles are passed out to students") was completed daily by the special education teacher to ensure the tootling procedures were followed correctly and the intervention was implemented as intended.

Results

In this section, the authors will describe the overall results of the case study. Specifically, how did tootling impact on-task behavior, disruptive behavior, and prosocial behavior within an EBD classroom? Before tootling was implemented, students' on-task behavior was exhibited in less than half of the observation intervals (43%) with a decreasing trend. In addition, students engaged in low levels of disruptive behavior (12.3%) and did not exhibit any instances of prosocial behavior (0%) during baseline sessions. Once the tootling intervention was implemented, students' on-task behavior increased to an average of 68% of observed intervals with a range from 57% to 87%. During the first intervention condition, there was little to no change in the students' disruptive behavior (13.33%) and prosocial behavior (0.33%). When the tootling intervention was withdrawn, a decreasing trend was observed for students' on-task performance with the level decreasing to an average of 51.5% of observed intervals (range from 43% to 67%). Students' disruptive behavior remained low (12%) while their prosocial behaviors remained near zero (0.5%). When the tootling intervention was reintroduced, students' on-task behaviors immediately increased, were variable, but remained above baseline levels (62%) throughout the phase. On-task behavior ranged from 43% to 83% of observed intervals. In addition, disruptive behavior (3.8%) immediately decreased and remained at low levels throughout the second phase of the tootling intervention. Students' prosocial behaviors (0.8%) remained close to zero levels during this condition. In summary, the results of this study demonstrate the effectiveness of the tootling intervention to both improve prosocial behavior and decrease inappropriate behavior in students with EBD.

Case Study #3: Tootling in a Special Education Resource Classroom

Mrs. Garcia was a teacher in an elementary self-contained special education classroom for students who need additional academic work time in order to be successful in school. She had 12 students in her class that range in age from six to nine years old. Students go to this classroom if they need additional time to complete their work or receive extra academic supports that is more than what is provided within the general education setting. Students in this class had a difficult time with stay on-task during their scheduled work time in the classroom. They engaged in many off-task conversations with each other, would work on something they were not supposed to, and would walk around the room when they were supposed to be working.

After several months of these consist off-task behaviors, she asked her school psychologist for help. Dr. Racciatti, the school psychologist, offered to come observe the students and see if she can offer any suggestions. Over the next week, Dr. Racciatti visited the classroom numerous times to determine why the students were continuously off-task, and what could be helpful to increase positive/appropriate behaviors in the classroom. She observes in the classroom for five days and from these observations comes up with several conclusions.

1   Dr. Racciatti notes that the students engage in off-task most often during the beginning of the class period and at the end of the class period. The

students tend to be more on-task during the middle of the class period when they are more engaged in the content.

2   When students are off-task, they are often engaging in conversations with other students in the classroom or attempting to get their teacher off-task.
3   When students are engaged in classwork, the staff tend to leave them alone and do other things like prepping for the next class period.
4   When the students are off-task and engaging in conversations with one another, the rest of the students in the class pay attention to them and also become off-task.
5   There were very little opportunities for the students in the classroom to interact positively when in the classroom due to the main focus being academic support.

Based on her observations, Dr. Racciatti decides that the students could benefit from the tootling intervention. She based this recommendation on the fact that the students seem very motivated by attention from adults and peers, and that the students get very little positive feedback when they are behaving appropriately. She feels that tootling would be a great way to increase the positive interactions between students and give the staff a structure for providing positive reinforcement to students when they interact positively.

Mrs. Garcia and Dr. Racciatti met to discuss the observations and Dr. Racciatti's recommendations. After explaining what tootling is and how to implement the intervention, the two women discuss the best way to implement tootling in this classroom. First, they discuss the tootle cards and what they will look like. Mrs. Garcia states that all most students in their classroom know how to read and write; however, expecting them to do this may be a challenge and could lead to less participation. It was decided to allow the students to write their name and their peer's name but to have checkboxes for specific positive behaviors observed. Dr. Racciatti asks Mrs. Garcia, which behaviors would she like to see from her students? She suggested that they focus on the most pressing behaviors first in order to see change as quickly as possible. Mrs. Garcia says that she understands that this intervention is designed to address social behavior, but she would also like to address interactions between students and staff and student academic behaviors. Based on this they decide to include the following behaviors on the tootle card

- Positive, on-task conversation with a peer
- Positive, on-task conversation with an adult
- Sharing
- Working on assigned tasks

In addition to these four choices, an "Other" line was also included so that students could write in their own examples of positive peer behavior.

Next, they needed to determine how to display the tootles in the classroom. Mrs. Garcia said that all the students in the class were really into football and wondered if they could find a way to incorporate that into the intervention. They decided to create a billboard in the classroom of a football field. Depending on the goal that was chosen for the number of tootles needed to earn a reward, a football player would be put on the field that many yards away from the goal line. For example, if the goal was 20 tootles the football player would be placed on the 20-yard line. Then, each day Mrs. Garcia would add up the number of tootles and move the player that many yards closer to a touchdown.

At this point they also decided to try to find a football shaped container that the students could put the tootle cards in after they were filled out. They also decided to include pictures of footballs on the tootle cards as well.

After Mrs. Garcia and Dr. Racciatti developed the materials for the intervention, they introduced the idea to the students. On Monday morning, the students came to school and saw the football billboard in the classroom. They were all curious about what the billboard is for and asked Mrs. Garcia about it. Dr. Racciatti and Mrs. Garcia explained to the students that they were going to start a new program in their class. Mrs. Garcia told the students that she wanted to focus on the students' positive behaviors and how they interact with each other. Mrs. Garcia and Dr. Racciatti explain to the students what tootling is and how it works. They discussed the behaviors that they would like to see from all of the students. They ask the students in the classroom to provide example of each of the behaviors listed above, as well as non-examples of the same behaviors. Then they explained to the students how to fill out the tootle cards and then role played examples of filling out the tootle cards.

Once they were sure that all the students understood how to write the tootles, they discussed the rewards. They told the students that there would be a goal for the number of tootles the class needs to write. When they meet that goal, the whole class will earn a reward. Mrs. Garcia had decided that the first goal would be low enough to reach within one day if all students wrote one tootle (12 tootles) in order to ensure the students earned a reward as quickly as possible. She knew that the kids in her class were very motivated by rewards and were more likely to buy into tootling if they were rewarded quickly. Dr. Racciatti explained to the students that each morning Mrs. Garcia would read the tootles in the box and add up how many tootles they had made the day before. If they had more tootles than the goal, they would earn a reward. If they didn't write that many tootles they could keep working toward their goal the next day. The tootles would accumulate until the reward was earned. The football player would help students to know how close they were to the goal.

Next, they asked the students to choose a reward. Mrs. Garcia had a pre-set list of possible rewards that she was comfortable with giving the students. She asked the students to choose from the list. Each student voted for their top choice and the item that received the most votes was chosen as the first reward. The students chose to have a flag football game at the end of the day for their first reward.

After this Mrs. Garcia handed out tootle cards to all of the students and told them to fill them out whenever they saw a peer doing one of the positive behaviors they discussed. She told them that they can fill out the tootle whenever they see one but should wait until the end of the class period to put the tootle in the tootle box.

Throughout the day, the students wrote tootles for their peers. Dr. Racciatti and Mrs. Garcia watched the students closely and pointed out appropriate behaviors that could be reported. This helped students to be more aware of the appropriate behaviors and increased the number of tootles that were written throughout the day.

At the end of the day, the students came to class and asked how many tootles they had written. Mrs. Garcia gathered the tootle cards out of the box and read several of them. The students clapped and cheered for their peers when the tootles were read. She then counted all of the tootles and moved the football player that many yards on the field. The goal had purposely been set very low in order to ensure that the class would earn a reward quickly. The goal was 12 tootles and the class had written 15. Since they met the goal, they had a 15-minute flag football game outside before they went home for the day.

Results

Over the course of the next few weeks, Mrs. Garcia raised the goal for the students multiple times. Dr. Racciatti visited the classrooms over that time and collected data in the same way she did prior to the start of intervention. She found that the students' on-task behavior increased from an average of 32% in baseline to 75% when tootling was in place. In addition, she noted that disruptive behavior was reduced from 20% to 5%. The students in the class reported that they really liked tootling. Most of the students said that it helped them to focus on what they should be doing rather than what they should not. The students had the opportunity to earn multiple rewards over the course of the next several weeks. They continued to choose flag football three or four times, until it started to get cold outside. After that, they requested basketball in the gym. Mrs. Garcia was happy to allow them to do this as it helped with physical activity, team work, and was a very powerful reinforcer that was resource friendly. She decided to keep tootling in place throughout the rest of the year, since it had been so helpful in increasing positive behavior and social interaction in the classroom.

Case Study #4: Tootling in a Social Skills Group

Ms. Sweeney has just started her first job as a social worker at middle school on the east coast. She recently graduated with her MSW, and is excited to begin working with the children at her new school. One of her many responsibilities is to conduct small group social skills groups with students at risk for social, emotional, and behavioral disorders. She has been assigned three social skills groups that she meets with three times a week. Based on conversations with classroom teachers, Ms. Sweeney has determined that the students in her morning group have adequate social skills, but that they do not always choose to use them with their classmates. Ms. Sweeney decides that she doesn't need to teach them how to interact with each other, but rather, should find a way to motivate the students to engage in positive social interactions. After reviewing research related to social skills interventions, Ms. Sweeney chooses the tootling intervention for her morning group. She feels this will be a perfect way to encourage the children to interact positively while in group.

When the children come to group for the first time, Ms. Sweeney introduces herself and let's the kids know that they will meet a few times a week to talk about the best ways to make friends and how to be a good friend. She lets them know that her office is a safe space and that, unless someone could get hurt or hurt someone else, anything they discuss in the group is confidential. She then says that they need to establish the rules for the group. Ms. Sweeney decided ahead of time that since these are middle school students, it would be a good idea to let them be a part of creating the rules and expectations for the group. This will give them a sense of ownership and allow them to express what is important to them.

After the rules have been established, she tells the students that they will be tootling in the group. She explains what tootling is and how it works. She explains to the students that they should pay attention and make note of whenever they see one of their friends being kind to another person. They talk about what it means to be kind and everyone gives examples. They also discuss what it means to be unkind, and why we want to avoid treating others poorly. After Ms. Sweeney is sure that the kids understand what they need to do, they decide on a tootle goal, then she starts her lesson. About 5 minutes before the end of the session, she asks the students if anyone had a tootle to share. Several of the students share observations they made of their peers being kind to one another during the lesson. Ms. Sweeney writes each tootle on the board, adds them up and determines if the students met the goal. She does this every time the children come to group. After a few weeks the classroom teachers of the kids in her group come to her and ask her to tell them about tootling. All of the kids love it and they seem to be getting along better with their peers. Ms. Sweeney works with several classroom teachers to get a tootling program up and running in their classrooms.

The examples provided above show the different ways that tootling can be implemented in a variety of settings. As you can see in each case, the essential components of the intervention (peer reporting, public posting, goal setting, and reinforcement) are present regardless of the situation. How each of these is implemented varies depending on the people and places involved.

As this book has shown, tootling is a simple, versatile intervention that can be used in a variety of settings with a wide range of children and adolescents. Implementation is easy with a minimal amount of training and experience with tootling. It can be adapted to meet the needs of students in all school-based settings, from the classroom to group intervention sessions. The implementation of tootling provides a proactive and positive approach to improving the prosocial skills of a wide range of students in school settings.

Index

Note: Locators in *italic* refer to figures; Locators followed by "n" indicate endnotes.